Grey and Silver Plants

Grey and Silver Plants

Mrs. Desmond Underwood

COLLINS
ST JAMES'S PLACE, LONDON

ISBN 0 00 214056 X

First published 1971
© Mrs. Desmond Underwood 1971

Printed in Great Britain
Collins Clear-Type Press
London and Glasgow

Contents

Illustrations

Preface

My interest in silver foliaged plants dates right back to a day just after the war, when, utterly frustrated by overwork and the general untidiness of a large border, I complained to my father that it was useless going on, for nothing would grow in a plot surrounded by a holly hedge and riddled with elm roots. Father had spent many years in Southern Europe and suggested quietly that I was going about things in quite the wrong way and that it would be better to forget all about Delphiniums and Lilies and concentrate instead on plants that knew how to withstand drought.

As a girl I had wandered over many of the foothills surrounding the Mediterranean and had often been sent clambering up cliffs collecting bits and pieces for the garden, so I had a hazy idea of the type of subject which grew on a hot bank. Unfortunately most of the names I was able to remember proved to be those of so-called half-hardy plants, which was somewhat discouraging. However, I was desperate and before long I had found out that many of these half-hardies could be overwintered on dry ground in Essex. Most of these plants were of course silver foliaged.

Very little had been written at the time about the peculiar requirements of silver foliaged plants, and to begin with it was a matter of trial and error. As the years passed so I grew to know what was likely to do well in my own patch and to wonder how these same plants might fare in other parts of the country and on different types of soil. Gardeners are a kindly breed and very soon I had accumulated a mass of notes on the behaviour of a number of silvers in all sorts of different areas.

Many friends have known about these notes and have been encouraging me to assemble them into a book. I doubt however whether I would ever have tackled the job had it not been for the inspiration of Marjorie Blamey's paintings. It had always seemed to me that the charm of grey leafed plants lay in the beauty of the texture of their leaves and that this was never captured in a photograph, but when I saw Marjorie's work I recognised that in some curious way she had managed to convey the 'feel' of the various leaves and to differentiate between felt, silk and velvet.

It would not be possible to mention all the many friends who have helped in so many ways, but my thanks are due to my publishers for all the trouble they have taken, and to Mrs. Morton for the many hours she has spent typing and re-typing the text. Above all though I owe a debt of gratitude to my secretary Kathleen Eichhorn who grows most of my favourite silvers and has taught me how well they can be managed by a busy working housewife.

Introduction

SILVER foliaged plants have been grown in English gardens for many years, but it is only recently that their true beauty has been fully appreciated. Although Miss Sackville-West, with her famous White Garden at Sissinghurst, was undoubtedly the originator of the 'silver' cult, I am sure that some of the interest must also stem from a lack of garden space combined with the enormous cost of paid labour.

The average garden nowadays is looked after by its owner as a part-time job. There is no time for messing about with bedding-plants or for growing tender treasures which need lifting every September. Even staking has become a chore which must be avoided at all costs. Furthermore, the vast majority of gardens these days are small and cannot afford the space for seasonal beds such as the early summer or late autumn borders of the inter-war years. The modern gardener wants the whole of the garden to be both tidy and beautiful at all times, and has begun to judge plants not merely for their flowers but also for their general effect when not in flower. From this line of thought to choosing a plant specifically for the beauty of its foliage is not a very big jump, and this surely accounts for the great increase in foliage plants grown, and for the popularity of 'silvers'.

Unfortunately there never was the garden which would grow every type of plant and some are certainly not suitable for any kind of grey. Contrariwise there are gardens where very little can be grown successfully except silvers!

These silver foliaged plants do not come from any particular family or genus, and in many cases it is only the odd species in a genus which has furry leaves. They are however all native to the dry and arid areas of the world, and are usually found on hot sunny slopes.

Plants that live on this sort of terrain are forced to adapt themselves to withstand long periods of drought. Some have thickened out their leaves and stems so that they can retain their moisture, but others, aiming at preventing loss through transpiration, have learnt to coat their leaves with a covering of wool, felt or silk. It is this covering, according to its density, which makes the leaves appear either silver or white.

Under cultivation a protective coating is only produced when there is a danger of a loss of moisture through the leaves. Both sun and wind can dry out the foliage and it is surprising how quickly green growth turns grey after a bright breezy day. On the other hand silvers that have been planted in the shade have a nasty habit of remaining dirty green throughout the summer.

Whether the waxy bloom which covers the leaves of so-called glaucous plants and makes them seem grey-blue is really intended to act in the same manner is unproven, but it would seem likely, for these plants need just as much sun and light as any of the true silvers.

By the sea, where the light is always more intense than it is inland, silvers and glaucous plants grow uncommonly well and go a good colour even when planted in semi-shade. They are, in fact, extremely useful plants for seaside gardens, as they do not seem to mind salt spray and positively enjoy a good blow.

The Artemisias and Helichrysum I have myself found on the slopes bordering the Mediterranean were always growing in what appeared to be arid conditions, although moisture could always be found a few inches below the surface. Whether this applies to the habitat of every silver-leafed subject I do not know, but experiments have certainly proved that while a pot plant of *Senecio cineraria* will grow happily on a wet bench the same plant will succumb if a wet rag is wrapped round the base of its stem. It would seem therefore that though the roots can tolerate a certain amount of wet the bark at the base of the stem rots very easily and should be kept as dry as possible. Winter casualties I have examined seem to confirm this theory. Death seldom occurs during frosty weather, but rather during a wet spell when the ground is covered with water or slush from melting snow, and it is always the base of the stem which rots first. Even quite tender plants seem to be able to withstand bitter weather if their bark is kept dry, and I shall always remember some discarded specimens of *Helichrysum petiolatum* which survived the winter of 1962–3 when thrown on to their sides on the rubbish heap. This was the hard winter and the thermometer registered 32 degrees of frost for one whole week. The rubbish heap stood out in the open and plants had been thrown on top. There was no reason why these tender plants should have survived except that the bark on their stems was kept completely dry.

Many gardens are difficult to drain and I am sure that the main reason why so many of the lovely Mediterranean silvers disappear during the winter is that the surface water does not always seep into the ground quickly enough and that the plants sometimes find themselves standing in puddles. How long they can survive this sort of discomfort I do not know, but I suspect that it may well be only a matter of minutes. Certainly the trial specimens were showing the first outward signs of distress less than an hour after the wet rags had been applied, and though the wrappings were removed from a couple of plants as soon as the first leaves started to droop, this was already too late and I was unable to resuscitate either patient.

Nothing, however, encourages a keen gardener more than to be told that a certain species is not for his garden, and I know of several who have drained their borders and incorporated a heavy dressing of sharp grit into the top spit. This must work well for there are some beautiful collections of silvers growing on the most unlikely land.

Although many silvers come from limestone formations and are probably a better colour when grown on lime it would appear that they can all do perfectly well without it, provided their site is suitably drained. At Glenveagh Castle in Eire, a representative collection was planted some years back in pure peat and has never given any trouble. Part of this garden, however, has to be watered in summer. Whether it would be as easy to grow silvers in many other peaty gardens in Eire is quite a different matter.

In towns pollution can cause trouble and before the days of the Clean Air Regulations it was not possible to grow even Lamb's Lug (*Stachys lanata*) in London. Things are better now, but there are still some patches near factories or power stations where industrial fall-out is a serious problem. Unfortunately the hairs and felt on the leaves attract and hold the dirt and this cannot be washed off. Densely felted subjects, such as *Senecio cineraria* 'White Diamond', should never be asked to overwinter in a polluted atmosphere, and are not really reliable in town gardens. On the other hand shrubs that are not so densely felted and therefore not so white, such as

Artemisia arborescens and *Santolina serratifolia*, often do as well in towns as they do in the country, whilst all the herbaceous perennials can be grown with impunity.

Luckily the hybridists have not yet started to play about with silver foliaged plants, and as far as I know nobody has tried to breed bigger or whiter leaves. Even the named cultivars such as *Senecio cineraria* 'White Diamond' are the result of selection rather than of deliberate hybridisation. Nevertheless there can be a considerable difference between individual specimens of the same variety, and some forms are very much better than others! This is easy to explain. In the wild there is always some variation of form according to habitat. This has been accentuated in cultivation by different gardeners choosing different types from which to propagate. Thus there are at least three distinct forms of *Artemisia lanata* to be found growing in this country, and one of these is not even grey!

The naming of many silver subjects is confused, and it is difficult to keep up with the changes. In some cases different forms of one variety were originally thought to be separate varieties. In other cases plants were introduced by several different collectors and received more than one name. These are gradually being sorted out, but unfortunately there are still a great number of varieties about which the experts disagree. In this book I have to a large extent followed common usage, but this may be very confusing to those who study labels in Botanical Gardens!

Garden dictionaries list a lot of plants with grey leaves, and when I first became interested in the type I imagined that there would be hundreds of different varieties to choose from. Actually, quite a few of those named do not seem to be obtainable in this country, or even in their own so-called country of origin, and a number of others, all with fascinating names and wonderful descriptions, have proved to be indistinguishable from my own favourites, or even worse, dreadfully disappointing.

There is all the difference in the world between the appearance of healthy plants and those that are sickly, and to be seen at their best most silvers need a little understanding. For this reason I propose to concentrate on the requirements and limitations of those plants which are readily obtainable and which I believe to be the best of their type. There are omissions, but I believe that it is wiser to discuss a few plants well rather than try to cover too much ground and include varieties which have never seemed to me to be 'garden worthy'. This is not a book for the botanist or for the plant snob who can only see beauty in the uncommon, but rather for the ordinary gardener who has grown tired of too much brilliance and needs a little peace.

CHAPTER I

Many Positions

DURING recent years, so-called 'grey borders' have become something of a status symbol, and many have been laid out in all parts of the country. I cannot help wondering whether they are really such a good idea, or whether their proud owners may not find them somewhat disappointing. Many years ago, inspired by the lovely white border at Sissinghurst – which, by the way, I saw on a bright day – I tried such a border myself but found it terribly depressing. It is true that there is a sufficiently wide range of shape and texture amongst the varieties available to give interest when the sun is shining, but in dull weather there is nothing particularly inspiring about a border which merely echoes the cold and gloom of a sullen sky.

Some gardeners like to think that they can rely for colour on the flowers produced by the silver plants themselves, but this does not work very well. To begin with, the flowers of most are nothing to write home about, and secondly, the actual effort of flowering has a very bad effect on the foliage and removes the lustre from the leaves. The early stage in the production of seed is a testing time for any plant and the brutal truth is that any shrub or perennial which has flowered will look shabby until it has made new growth. However, all the different shades of grey make perfect foils for colour and just a few flowers intermingled with the silvers make all the difference. Hybrid pinks are an idea for this purpose. Some varieties flower for months on end and their glaucous foliage would justify a position in any grey border!

Although 'white' types with heavily felted foliage, such as *Senecio cineraria* 'White Diamond' or *Tanacetum densum amanum*, are extremely showy, it is a mistake to concentrate entirely on them and to ignore the true 'silvers' and the 'grey-blues'. A border planted entirely with 'white' foliage would be a very flat affair and the contrast of different greys is needed for depth. Furthermore, although 'white' makes a perfect backcloth for pastel coloured flowers, scarlet and crimson are much more effective when seen against glistening silver.

Some varieties will grow to 5 ft. or more, but it is better not to choose silver or white leaved shrubs for a position in which height is needed unless the plant concerned is going to be seen from above. Anyone who has seen an unpruned specimen of *Senecio laxifolius* will probably have noticed that, however dull and dreary the shrub may appear, there are always some beautiful sprigs on top where the growth is exposed to the full light. The same can be said of *Artemisia arborescens*. The joy of this particular Artemisia is that it seems to shimmer on a bright day. This effect is caused by the reflection of light from the silky hairs covering the leaves, and it is only those leaves which catch the light that shimmer. Ideally, I suppose, we should all plant our silvers at the bottom of a flight of steps and then they could be encouraged to grow to their full height, but, for those who do not own terraced gardens, the best course is to keep the plants pruned back and rely on biennials such as *Onopordon arabicum* or *Verbascum bombicyferum* for any height needed.

Curiously enough, although the bushy types lose so much of their splendour when seen from underneath, the dwarf alpines, such as *Artemisia lanata pedemontana*, *Antennaria aprica* and *Tanacetum densum amanum*, make the most attractive carpets for steep banks. These banks are always perniciously dry, but this does not seem to worry these varieties and, once they have grown into one another, the effect is reminiscent of a sunny slope overlooking the Mediterranean. Slightly taller Artemisias and Helichrysums can be used to break the flatness, and if colour is needed, it is well to know that there are many forms of Dianthus, including the so-called Miniatures, which can stand the same dry conditions.

Although properly constructed rockeries should not need any carpeting, a scattering of silver is a welcome sight once the majority of Alpines are past their best. The Royal Botanic Gardens in Edinburgh have a very interesting collection and this may be one reason why the famous rock garden is so popular with the general public in July despite a general lack of colour, for the various misty greys blend well with the rocks and focus attention on the last remaining flowers.

True plant lovers often find that a carefully planned mixed border has deteriorated into a glorified pet's corner. It is fatally easy to acquire a mixed assortment of treasures and push them all into the border. This eventually loses all form and cohesion, and gives the impression of always being past its best. One way of overcoming a lack of unity without interfering with precious plants is to tidy up the front edge with a carpet of those silvers recommended for banks. The edge is always the hottest and driest part of any border, and perfect for dwarfs such as Tanacetums, Achilleas and low growing Artemisias. This alone will help but the general effect can be further improved if space can be found inside the bed for a few specimen greys. These shrubby subjects are not gross feeders, and are unlikely to starve their neighbours, which cannot be said for some of the herbaceous types such as *Artemisia ludoviciana* which has a very nasty habit of throttling anything valuable!

This idea of interplanting can be carried much further when a new border is being planned and drifts of grey can be so placed that they will camouflage any gaps left after the early flowering border plants have had their day. This makes it possible to grow things like Lupins and Delphiniums and yet have a furnished border in late summer and autumn. Again it is the front edge which matters. If this can be kept tidy and attractive a few gaps will never be noticed.

The contrast between silver and green is interesting, and many an old shrub border would be given a face lift if only a few clumps of silver foliaged shrubs were introduced. Unfortunately this is not always possible because so many of these old borders lack light. Old-fashioned and shrub roses, on the other hand, usually stand in open positions, and it is well worth planting a varied selection of grey at their feet. Soft greys harmonise well with the roses when they are flowering, and prevent the border looking quite so forlorn when the rose display is over.

Artemisias with invasive roots are not really suitable for mixed borders but come into their own when an odd patch of rough soil has to be covered in a hurry. They can also be grown quite close to the trunks of deciduous trees such as apples or cherries. Other useful subjects which can be planted on the sunny side of these trees include *Anaphalis triplinervis, Stachys lanata* and *Ballota pseudodictamnus*, while *Acaena adscendens*, one of the New Zealand burrs can always be relied on to cover an ugly patch of soil however poor the ground.

Weeding was never a popular pastime. In recent years a great deal has been written about the value of ground cover, but unfortunately everyone seems to have a different idea of what constitutes a good ground covering plant, and many are recommended for the purpose which I would have thought unsuitable. The average carpeting type is of little value, for it is not really tall enough to smother weeds. The ideal must surely be a plant which is so dense that when a weed does manage to establish itself it is starved of light and therefore cannot mature properly. This is the theory, but in practice there will always be the occasional weed which will manage to grow a fine root before it is spotted, and so I think that it is just as important to pick out plants which have a strong root system, so that weeds can be removed without doing damage. Good silvers for ground covering include all the Santolinas, *Helichrysum angustifolium*, *Anaphalis triplinervis*, and Ballota. They are not necessarily very short, but they can keep down weeds.

The very fact that silvers do not require much soil or water makes them the perfect subjects for window boxes and roof gardens. It would of course be unwise to try them in the shade, but it may be useful to remember that of all plants those with grey leaves are the best adapted to stand wind and draught, and that they can be relied on to remain healthy in conditions which would daunt many so-called 'hardies'.

CHAPTER 2

Hardy or Delicate

GREY foliaged plants belong to many families and come from all sorts of climates. It is therefore not surprising that they differ in their ability to withstand the rigours of our winters. The question of hardiness is controversial, but I have never been able to understand why those who would never expect a Rhododendron to survive on chalk should automatically label the Mediterranean Senecios 'half-hardy' just because they cannot tolerate badly drained ground. There are, of course, some species and varieties which must be treated as tenders. These originate in the main from Australia and Teneriffe, but a great many of the best silvers come from the hills surrounding the Mediterranean and the Adriatic and these are seldom damaged by frost except in late spring when they are carrying a lot of immature green growth.

The importance of good drainage cannot be over-emphasised however. That constant wet is far more deadly than frost is borne out by a comparison between the losses sustained during the winter of 1961–2 and those of 1968–9. In the notorious 'hard winter' the cold came after a comparatively dry summer and autumn and though the land was eventually frozen to a depth of three feet for weeks on end, there were few casualties. By contrast, in 1968 a wet autumn succeeded an even wetter summer and the ground was saturated throughout the winter. No particularly severe frosts were recorded but all the silver-foliaged plants suffered to some degree, and some did not recover.

It would have been all too easy to blame the hard frosts in February and March for this disaster, and to have decided that the varieties which succumbed were not sufficiently hardy for this climate, but it happens that most of the shrubs were found dead in November, and I imagine that the missing perennials probably collapsed at the same time.

Some years ago I found an old *Artemisia arborescens* fighting its way through a tangle of brambles in a deserted garden in the heart of Northamptonshire. This is not a shrub which one would expect to enjoy the wet clammy cold of Midland clay, and I was not surprised to be told that it had once been treated as something very precious and had always spent the winters in a peach house. At first sight it seemed unbelievable that such a delicate plant could have been able to fend for itself in such an unsuitable part of the world, for it was doubtful whether the top growth of the brambles would have been much protection. However, when I examined the site more carefully, I found that it had originally been set on top of a steep six-foot bank, which had gradually been taken over by bramble roots. Anyone who has had to clear such a bank will probably remember that the top three inches of soil were very dry indeed, and so it was in this case, although it was raining at the time and the rest of the garden was unpleasantly wet.

Brambles are not particularly good at removing surplus water from the soil in which they grow, and it was of course the steep slope which accounted for the dryness round the root of the old Artemisia. Nevertheless it is interesting to notice how many of the more delicate silvers seem to prefer living within the range of hungry roots. Elms and Silver Birches have a very bad reputation for removing food and moisture from borders, but they certainly do not damage silver-foliaged subjects.

Latitude and longitude seem to make very little difference, and silvers will prove as hardy in the North as they will in the South provided they are given a sunny position and a well drained root run. This was proved when identical collections were planted in Angus and in Sussex. The gardens chosen for the experiment were very similar, both standing on hills about a mile from the sea, but whereas the ground in Scotland was light and sandy I had managed to find a really heavy bit of land in Sussex, and knew that it had not been double dug. The plants sent to Angus got away to a quick start and weathered the winter without trouble. There were in fact some very pleasant surprises, for the long nights and short days of a Scottish winter had not upset even the Mediterranean varieties. In Sussex however the story was quite different. The plants had to be coaxed into growth and were still far too small in September. After a month of autumn rain they all looked utterly miserable, and many were dead before Christmas. In spring I was forced to admit that the only reliable silvers for unworked clay were *Artemisia purshiana* and *Achillea* 'Moonshine'. Hardly a big selection!

Unfortunately there is a lot of clay in this country and many gardeners have to compete with soil which is by no means ideal. There is however clay and well worked clay, and there are some silvers which are more tolerant than others. For some years I have been trying – with the help of many friends – to find out which these are, and how much drainage each variety required. This has involved sending plants to differing soils in various parts of the country and recording their subsequent behaviour. The results suggest that a heavy rainfall is only dangerous on heavy ground and that one should not assume that because a certain plant comes from a warm country it will necessarily need protection or even ideal conditions. *Helichrysum splendidum* and *Artemisia nutans* are two very good examples of plants which can adapt themselves, for both will flourish on well worked heavy soil in Derbyshire although they actually come from South Africa and Corsica.

Unexpected failure with types which should be perfectly hardy can often be traced to the strain planted. Although the silvers normally seen in this country are not 'alpine', in any true sense of the word, they do originate from hilly slopes and there is often a considerable variation not only in the appearance of the strains but also in their hardiness. Thus plants grown from seed collected at a high altitude will always be hardier than those raised from seed collected lower down. It is therefore perfectly possible to find that though one strain of *Artemisia lanata* is useless another may be perfectly hardy. One of these days we may even see the Californian *Lupinus ornatus* in our gardens again. This lovely little shrub, with its brilliant silver leaves and pale blue flowers, was grown as a hardy in many pre-war gardens and though it was not considered to be very long lived no special precautions were ever taken to protect it. In those days we propagated it from our own seed but the strain was lost during the war years. Nowadays, alas, *Lupinus ornatus* has to be treated as a half hardy, and I am sure that it is the seed which is at fault.

Even when the original strain is hardy it can still be undermined by careless propagation, and this applies more especially to varieties which have to be increased either by cuttings, layers or division. These are, after all, merely small parts of the original parent forced to produce new roots, and must therefore carry all the vices and virtues of their parent throughout life. Even among the very hardiest varieties it is sometimes possible to find an isolated specimen which feels the winter more than it should, and always gets badly cut back. Youngsters raised from this sort of parent are never really satisfactory. On the other hand the converse is equally true and it is sometimes possible to improve the stamina of a delicate subject by propagating from an individual which has proved its ability to adapt itself to life in an unsuitable position. Just as certain humans can learn to adjust to different conditions a lot better than others so can the occasional plant, and one does come across the odd specimen which has no right to be doing as well as it is and which makes a marvellous parent!

CHAPTER 3

Propagation

THE difference in the appearance and decorative value of different specimens of the same variety can often be traced back to the treatment the plants received when young, for it is difficult to do much for a plant which has had a bad start. One reason for this is that the roots of most plants find it difficult to change tempo and, once forced to slow down, seldom regain their momentum. On the other hand, when the roots of a young plant have been encouraged to develop steadily, they will continue in the same manner when planted in the open border. This is not to suggest that young silvers should either be forced or overfed, but rather that the propagation of these plants is worth doing properly, for good specimens are not raised on neglect.

Very few silver shrubs or perennials are deliberately raised from seed, partly because seed is difficult to obtain and does not always ripen in this country, but mainly because the results are so variable. Some self-sown seedlings do develop into worthwhile specimens but this does not happen very often and it is as well to make certain that the foliage is up to standard before giving such a plant a prominent position.

Monocarpic plants, on the other hand, are generally grown from seed. When the seedlings are intended to run to flower in the following summer, seed should be set in the open ground in June or early July and the plants transferred to their permanent quarters in early September. Plants that are not intended to flower can be sown in August or at any time from March onwards, and flower decorators often sow a few seeds every fortnight throughout spring and summer so as to maintain a continuity of cuttable leaves. Most seed germinates reasonably well if it is not covered too deeply, but care must be taken at lifting time to see that the roots are prised carefully out of the ground. Unfortunately, slugs seem to prefer these seedlings to any other form of food or bait and the seed-bed must always be protected by cinders.

Because slugs are so tiresome it is sometimes more convenient to sow indoors and transfer the seedlings into 3″ pots. For ordinary garden purposes sufficient seed can be set in a plastic sandwich box filled to within 1″ of the top with one of the new soil-less composts which are sold damp. If the lid is put back on the box after the seed is covered and lightly pressed the compost will not dry out, even when brought into the house. This is a fascinating method of raising seed and one which delights children. It is also remarkably reliable provided the box is not left in a hot or sunny position. Some condensation may occur and the lid may have to be wiped, but otherwise there is nothing to do except wait for the appearance of the first seedling when the box must be uncovered and moved into the light.

There is a lot to be said in favour of transferring seedlings into pots before they have developed their first true leaf for at this stage the root merely consists of a straight thread which can be eased out of the compost without injury. Pots are preferable to boxes as the damage done when the roots have to be disentangled at planting time is often sufficient to unbalance the seedlings.

Soil-less composts are convenient but it is not necessary to fill the pots with anything very elaborate when they are going to be used for a very short period, and these monocarpic seedlings will do perfectly well in any open mixture, such as one consisting of equal parts of garden loam and sand.

Once the seedlings are established in their pots the first true leaves develop rapidly and it is then possible to pick out and discard those that are not carrying sufficient felt or wool. These are usually much larger than average seedlings and would develop into ugly green rogues.

Careful watering is important, for though the roots would be checked if the soil were allowed to dry out, too much water is fatal. For the first few days it is sufficient to keep the leaves fresh by spraying, but afterwards the surface of the soil must always be damped down a few minutes before the plants are given their full ration. This ensures that the water given goes down to the base of the pots where it is needed.

There is no point in keeping the plants in their pots a moment longer than necessary and once the root fibres have reached the side of the pots the seedlings do better in the open border. They will, however, still be attractive to slugs and should be ringed with cinders.

For those with glass, shrubby silvers are easy to propagate, for they root readily from soft cuttings. For those without, it is better to layer or to rely on half mature cuttings taken in July and covered with some form of cloche. On the whole, silvers do not strike well from hard wood, although this does not apply to some Santolinas and Lavenders.

It is not difficult to find the right type of semi-hard cutting in July. The shoots to choose are side-breaks from the main lead and must be firm rather than sappy. These cuttings do not need any bottom heat but root best when they are taken off the parent with a heel or wafer-like slice of old wood and bark. Cuttings should always be taken in the early morning when the parent plants are still full of vitality, but they wilt quickly and cannot be left lying about. Before insertion the heel must be trimmed clean with a sharp knife or razor and all lower leaves removed.

Rooting can take place in a frame or in a border, provided the position chosen is open to the light but protected from the sun, as the leaves will tend to flag in the sun until a callous has formed at the base of the cutting.

There is some evidence that cuttings strike quicker when the rooting surface lies close to the side of the clay pot and it is certainly more convenient to strike silvers in 5″ pots rather than in the open ground, for once the plants have started to root, they go ahead better in a brighter position. However, the pots must be well crocked and eventually sunk into the ground so that moisture is conserved. The best compost for striking silvers is one that is both gritty and open. Pure sharp sand is probably the best but this should only be used if the plants can be potted the moment they root as there is no food in sand and the plants can starve very quickly if neglected. As a compromise, a mixture of equal parts loam, peat and sand can be pressed down on the crocks and covered with an inch of sharp sand.

The actual setting is a matter of moments. A hole is made with a dib cut to the thickness required for the shoot. This should be fairly near the side of the pot so that the base of the shoot lies against the clay when it has been inserted to a depth of about an inch. Firming must be gentle but it is important to make sure that the sand round the base is carefully consolidated. A 5″ pot will usually take seven cuttings, and when all have been inserted, a light tap on the bench will level off the surface. Watering-in serves to consolidate the medium but the cuttings should not be given too much water thereafter as they will not use much until they have rooted and roots do not develop in a wet medium.

If the cuttings are left uncovered they will need constant spraying to counteract the drying effect of the wind, but this can be avoided if the pots are covered with closed cloches or even with two-pound jam jars. These, of course, do collect condensation and will have to be wiped every morning, but they can be removed as soon as the first signs of new growth can be seen, for this means that callousing has occurred.

July cuttings should be ready by September but this is not a good time to put babies into the open ground so it is better to pot individually into 3″ pots and keep the plants in a sunny frame for the winter. This time the compost is important, for though the young plants are unlikely to use much food during the dark months of winter, it must be remembered that they will have to stay in their pots for at least seven months. Perhaps the best answer is to pot into a standard J.I. No. 1 mixture or an equivalent soil-less compost. This will carry the plants through to the middle of March when a light feed of Bio can be given and repeated at fortnightly intervals. In a normal year this routine should be adequate, but healthy plants can consume a lot of food when the weather is bright and it is sometimes necessary to pot on into 6″ pots in order to prevent starvation and premature flowering.

Air is as essential for the health of the young plants as food and they must not be coddled. Nevertheless it is wise to put on the lights when the weather is frosty and when it is raining. Excess wet will do much more damage in winter than any cold, but once the growth starts in spring the plants need quite a lot of water and will come to no harm if left standing in the rain for a while.

Soft cuttings taken in June are more pernickety but root well if supplied with all their creature comforts. They are, of course, much more inclined to wilt than semi-hard cuttings and need bottom heat, but it is not so necessary to take them with a heel. Silvers are not the perfect subjects to root in mist as their foliage holds the moisture and thus attracts botrytis. If a mist frame is used the control must be set to 'Wean' so that the mist does not come on too frequently. As a further precaution, cuttings that are going into mist must always be dusted or sprayed with a fungicide, such as Thiram or Orthocide. It takes a little longer to strike cuttings in a perfectly ordinary closed frame with bottom heat and it is certainly not so effortless: the glass covering has to be wiped down each day, the cuttings themselves will need hand-spraying and the frame may have to be shaded when the sun is out and uncovered when the sky is grey. All this is troublesome, but the results are probably worth while, for it is a lot easier to wean silvers that have been rooted fairly dry than those that have been in the equivalent of a rain forest.

In June the shoots are seldom more than five inches long and must be trimmed to just below a joint or to a heel if this is more convenient. They strike best in pure sharp sand and can be inserted into 5″ pots in the same way as the semi-hard cuttings. If the pot is sunk into the bed, one good watering-in after insertion should keep the sand moist for a few days.

The aftercare of these June cuttings is much the same as for semi-hard growth but it must be remembered that plants which are taken from bottom heat are always somewhat soft, while those taken from mist will wilt badly when removed from the frame. This is a very good reason for rooting in pots as the young plants can be hardened off for a couple of days before having to undergo the ordeal of repotting. Even so, if the weather happens to turn hot when the plants are being potted, their leaves will droop and the only way of preventing this is to shade and spray fairly frequently.

The great advantage of these soft wood cuttings is that if they are kept growing in their pots, they should be ready for the open border in July and therefore have a good chance of making wood before the winter. To achieve this, however, they must be kept steadily growing and this means careful watering. No one can say how often a young plant must be watered in summer. In dull weather it may only want water every third day, but when the sun is bright it may well want a drink three times a day! In any case it is important to make sure that the water really does get down to the bottom of the pot and does not merely damp the surface.

The sooner a young shrub can be stopped the better, for as it goes on growing upwards so the lower leaves start to droop, and once a leaf has actually withered away the bud which lies between it and the stem dies and the plant is then unable to force a break out of that particular node. This means that a plant which has been neglected will always be leggy because it will have no breaks near the base. Generally speaking shrubs should be stopped as soon as it is possible to take off the tip and two pairs of leaves and leave three or four nodes on the plant.

The breaks usually emerge within a few days of stopping and develop rapidly. Once they are in full growth the original leaves begin to droop. This often worries gardeners, but is perfectly normal. The old leaves have done their job and from now on it is the shoots which matter to the plant.

Although most dwarf silvers can be increased, either by cuttings or division, it is not always necessary to do anything in order to obtain more plants as many varieties produce adventitious roots on their stems and one can usually find some pieces which have rooted into the ground and can be detached. When extra plants are needed of these varieties it is merely a question of pressing a handful of soil down on to a lead and waiting for a few weeks for the roots to appear. This is the simplest form of layering, but layering is, in any case, quite the simplest and most trouble-free method of propagation as, once the initial work has been done, little aftercare is needed.

The best time to layer silvers is in late June or early July when the young wood is pliable and there is still time for the roots to form before autumn. With pruned plants there should be plenty of shoots growing outwards from the base and it sometimes simplifies the actual job if some of these are encouraged to grow parallel with the ground while they are still soft in June.

Layers can be struck in the ground round the plants if this is loosened and mixed with sand, or they can be pegged down into sunken pots filled with soil-less compost. The latter method is probably the quickest but there seems to be little difference in the end products! How much sand to put into the ground is dependent on the type of soil, but the mixture should be at least fifty-fifty unless the land is known to be particularly light. The moisture content of the soil is important, for though layers will not root in a powder-dry medium, it is quite impossible to secure them firmly in newly watered soil. If the ground must be watered, it is therefore best to do this at least two days ahead and cover the wet soil with dry crumbs of earth.

It is seldom possible to produce a big specimen from a layer of a silver-foliaged plant for most of the leads are too short and the incision usually has to be made somewhere about eight inches from the tip. This only leaves the top three pairs of leaves clear when the layer is pegged down. All the other leaves must be removed.

The stems of most silvers tend to be brittle even in June and it takes a lot of patience to shape them so that they can be secured with their tips erect. Flower decorators know that quite hard wood can be shaped by pinching and stroking and the same technique will often help to bring down an obstinate stem. This is the only difficult part for the actual cutting of the so-called tongue is easy and merely consists of making an upward cut from underneath a joint with a very sharp knife. The incision must pass through the bark on the underside of the shoot into the wood of the stem and extend upwards for about an inch and a half, but the knife must never be allowed to pass into the centre of the wood. The tongue is then wedged open and firmly secured into the ground with a layering pin or a large hair pin, care being taken to see that the tongue is kept open as it comes into contact with the soil. Finally a mound of earth some 6″ deep is thrown round the layer and consolidated before being watered.

Once the roots have formed the layer can be severed from the parent. It is now a self-supporting plant which should be as hardy as its parent but no hardier! So, if the parent is known to be capable of overwintering in the border, the young plant should be left in situ until spring when it can be moved to its permanent position. When there is any doubt as to hardiness, however, it is safer to pot and keep the layer in a dry frame for the winter.

Most grey leaved perennials will root from cuttings taken in early spring and it is perfectly feasible to use the shoots removed at thinning time for the purpose. The other way of increasing these plants is by division. This is very satisfactory when properly carried out and when the worn-out centre of each stool is firmly discarded. Unfortunately one often sees ragged plants which are the result of replanting a mixture of young and old growth. It should never be necessary to use a spade to divide the pieces as those that are suitable lie round the outside of the stool and can be prised off without difficulty. How big each piece should be is a matter of choice and, of course, of variety. I have often found that it helps to count the buds that can be seen on the roots and visualise what these will look like when they have grown into stems, always remembering that the plants will never be so handsome if they are overcrowded.

Silver perennials can be divided in October or in March according to convenience, but whenever the job is done, it is as well to get the pieces back into the ground just as soon as possible, for it does not take long for the buds to dry out and shrivel, and once this has happened the plant has to work very hard to repair the damage.

Plants with fleshy roots can usually be propagated from root cuttings but the roots of most silver shrubs are fibrous rather than fleshy and those perennials which do have the right kind of root are easy enough to propagate by division so the only time it is worth worrying about this form of propagation is when one wants to increase some particular biennial or monocarpic plant which will not come true from seed and which is known to be difficult to strike from cuttings. *Verbascum domulosum* is a good example. A true plant is a real treasure seldom growing more than twenty inches and capable of flowering for months on end. Unfortunately it is distinctly promiscuous and seedlings often grow to four foot. Sometimes it is possible to root the shoots that spring from the base of the plant but the cuttings usually go to flower before they have even rooted, so root cuttings are really the only answer. The root must, of course, be in prime condition if the cuttings are to strike and this means that the plant must not be carrying any seed at all. The parent, of course, has to be dug up and the root divided into two-inch pieces which are inserted into a sandy compost. They do best when inserted vertically about an inch below the surface and with that part of the root which was nearest the stem uppermost. In order to recognise which is top, and which is tail, it is usual to cut the bottom of the piece diagonally and the top flat.

It is probable that we are not sufficiently adventurous with root cuttings and that there are other plants that would be easier to propagate in this manner. Certainly *Romneya coulteri*, the Californian Poppy, will grow from root cuttings if these are laid horizontally into sandy compost and I have been told that *Convolvulus cneorum* will respond. The only trouble is that though the occasional broken root will produce a perfectly good shoot and grow into a beautiful plant, when I take the trouble to make a proper root cutting it withers away instantly! Probably it is a question of time of year rather than mere cussedness.

CHAPTER 4

Preparing and Planting

ALTHOUGH many gardeners prefer putting out their shrubs and herbaceous perennials in autumn, experience has taught me that the only silvers that should be planted in the back end are those biennials, such as *Onopordon arabicum* and *Verbascum bombicyferum*, that need time to enable them to run up to flower.

In theory, there should be no reason why herbaceous perennials, such as *Achillea* 'Moonshine', *Artemisia purshiana* or *Veronica incana* should not be put out in October or November. These are all hardy and appear to have the kind of root system which one would expect to be able to cope with winter conditions. In practice, however, they make no progress whatsoever and merely develop lazy habits from which they do not recover. Perhaps they need a warm root run for I have often noticed that plants put out in April make better progress than those set out in March.

With shrubs, on the other hand, there is a sound reason for holding back young plants till May, for they do not become frost-resistant until they have outgrown their sappy stage and have produced some wood at the base. The wood of second year specimens is, of course, usually fairly ripe, but even here little is gained by autumn planting, for the roots of silver-foliaged plants are never very active in cold soil and always wait till April before starting to work.

Summer planting can be very successful, which makes it possible to use these shrubs for filling those tiresome gaps which appear in every border at some stage. Of course small specimens cannot be expected to make much show in their first year, and for this purpose it is better to choose second year plants, which are easy to establish and develop quickly.

The aim when preparing a plot for any kind of plant must be to try and copy its natural environment as much as possible. In this case this means that the ground needs to be both poor and well drained. Funnily enough at the start silvers will appear to flourish in a rich loam, but because the growth is so fast they never get a chance either to produce a protective cover for their leaves or even the essential wood. Hence they are neither attractive nor even hardy when grown on well fed soil, and the only hope on rich land is to plant them in pockets of sand or grit.

This is easy, but it is much more difficult to correct bad drainage, and no silver will tolerate being kept constantly wet in winter. Perhaps the best time to assess the suitability of a border is when the snow is melting. If a heavy fall disappears into the ground without trace it can be assumed that all is well, but if the snow leaves behind a sticky mess of mud, steps must be taken to persuade the water to run down into the ground and not merely remain on the surface.

The most common cause of bad drainage is a hard pan or crust lying under the top soil. Water cannot get through this and therefore builds up on the surface. In the days of trenching and double digging it was unusual to find such a pan in a garden, but in this generation borders are often prepared either with a rotovator or some similar mechanical tool, and thereafter merely forked, so that the sub-soil is never properly broken up. This would not matter if there were plenty of worms present, for they are quite capable of doing all the sub-soiling necessary, but one seldom finds a good worm population in neglected ground. Double digging is really the most satisfactory method of breaking up a pan when the border is needed for silvers. It is possible to attract a working population of worms to a plot with a heavy dressing of organic material, but this tends to make the soil too rich.

On heavy land it is not sufficient just to break down the sub-soil, for the roots of most grey-foliaged subjects thoroughly dislike finding themselves incarcerated in sticky clay. When preparing for a number of plants it pays to remove some of the clay whilst double digging, and to replace it with a three inch layer of crocks or stones. The top may also need attention, especially if it is very lumpy. Peat is excellent for making heavy soil workable and does no harm to the silvers, but grit or sand should always be added at the same time to prevent lush growth.

Despite the fact that grey foliaged plants are lime-loving they can be grown perfectly well on acid soil, though there is some evidence that the density of the hairs and felt on their leaves may be governed by the amount of lime present. I am always dubious about advising anyone to put lime on to ground which might, at some future date, be needed for Azaleas or Camellias, and I believe it wrong to add lime in the first year. Thereafter, if the plants are not sufficiently grey, limestone chippings, often sold as chicken grit, can be added as a dressing. These chippings are about the size of a currant and practically insoluble. When they are forked into the top three inches of soil it has been found that the root fibres of lime-lovers will wrap themselves round individual chippings and are thus able to absorb all the lime they require. On the other hand because the chips are so hard there is little danger of any quantity of lime being washed down into the subsoil where it might damage the wandering roots of some lime-hater. It must, however, be recognised that limestone chippings are remarkably persistent and that a patch which has once been dressed with them will not grow Rhododendrons or Azaleas for a very long time.

The eventual development of all plants is dependent on how quickly they can force their roots out into the surrounding soil, and here it must be emphasised that roots which have started to circle round and round a ball of soil find it very difficult to get out of the bad habit. This is one reason why a pot-bound plant will stand still for weeks on end. The right time to plant is when the fibres have reached the sides of the pot and have just started to wind round the ball of soil. If it is inconvenient to put the plant out when this stage has been reached the only answer is to pot it on into a larger pot, for pot-bound specimens are always a nuisance. Once the roots have become tangled it is usually too late to do much, for the plants themselves will have become badly starved. Ideally all such plants should be discarded, but very precious specimens can be helped by root-pruning, re-potting and foliar feeding with Liquid Seaweed.

Root development is also influenced by the moisture content of the ball of soil at the time of planting, as the root fibres have little chance of escaping into the ground around them if this is either too dry or too wet. Plants that have been watered at night are usually in perfect condition the next morning.

Droughts are common in late spring and early summer and, though grey-leaved plants do not need much moisture, they certainly get off to a better start if their roots are surrounded by moist soil. This often means 'puddling-in' and, though this may seem a tiresome job at the time, it does save subsequent watering when properly done. A hole dug out to a depth of six inches will absorb about a gallon of water, which is enough to keep the roots going until the plant is well established. Again this should be done overnight as it is impossible to plant firmly in mud.

The original ball of soil must never be buried. This is important as it is the bark at the base of the stem which is most vulnerable to rot. It is however just as important to plant firmly, making sure that the soil is well packed round the sides of the ball. Firm planting is emphasised in every book on gardening, but the results of careless planting are not always underlined. It is of course obvious that it cannot be good for the health of a plant to be rocked in the wind, but not quite so obvious that a loose plant will always dry out because its ball of soil is surrounded by bubbles of air instead of solid earth.

Firm planting will prevent any serious loss of moisture from the root, but it cannot prevent transpiration during hot or windy weather, and for this reason the plants should really be mulched as soon as they are planted. This will conserve the moisture in the ground so that there is always something to draw on. Ordinary mulches are unsuitable as they hold the moisture during wet weather, but a scattering of stones or pebbles is very effective.

It is possible to keep silver shrubs in 8″ pots for the whole of their lives, planting them into the border each spring, and lifting them in autumn. This is probably not such a tedious business as it sounds and is certainly the only way of growing some of the more exciting subjects on ground that cannot be properly drained. The young plants can be potted at any time before planting, and no special compost is required providing the pots are well crocked. There is no need to bring them under cover for the winter so long as a position can be found that is dry and sunny. If this is out of the wind the plants are unlikely to require watering in winter, and in fact must be left fairly dry. In spring, however, when the growth starts to show they may need water for a few weeks, but should be returned to the border as soon as the surface starts to 'hazel'. After a couple of years the soil inside the pots may need changing. Larger pots are seldom required but some root pruning is usually essential, and for this reason repotting is safer in spring.

Post and rail consignments sometimes arrive in bad shape and though all reputable nurserymen will replace if they are informed straight away, this takes time and there is always the unpleasant possibility that the second parcel may fare no better than the first.

Luckily the damage is seldom as serious as it would appear at first sight and a great deal can be done by prompt First Aid. It is usually the length of time in transit which causes trouble rather than physical damage. However carefully the parcel may have been packed there is always the danger that some of the plants may have been either too wet or too dry, for there is very little tolerance. After a week plants that were too wet will overheat, whilst the potting compost will crumble away from those that were too dry, leaving the roots completely bare.

When soil has been used for potting some of the root fibres may get torn away with the crumbs. This can affect the future development of the plant, but most nurserymen these days use soil-less composts and these merely fall away leaving the roots intact and capable of functioning again once the plants are repotted and watered. As soon as the tips of the leaves are turgid and signs of fresh growth can be seen the patients can be put out into the open border.

Overheating seldom does much harm to varieties with strong foliage, but those with fine silky leaves, such as *Artemisia schmidtiana*, often suffer badly and lose all their leaves. However dreadful they may look, many can be brought back to life, but they must first be carefully cleaned and then sprayed with Orthocide. The plants must not be planted out until they have started to show signs of recovery, but stood in an open position out of the direct rays of the sun. They are unlikely to require much water for the first few days but should not be allowed to dry out completely. If the treatment is going to succeed breaks will appear within a week at each leaf axil.

No chapter on planting would be complete without a very serious warning about birds. In certain areas sparrows have become a menace, and though they do little permanent damage to established plants even when they decide to line their nests with a few furry leaves, the havoc they create when they find a newly planted group of silvers has to be seen to be believed. It often seems that the poor plants are attacked just because they are strangers in the land!

I have always been a firm believer in black cotton, for when properly strung it definitely stings the birds if they fly into it, and this undoubtedly acts as a deterrent. However, black cotton is useless unless it is taut, and this means driving several stakes firmly into the ground so that they will hold when the cotton is strained from one to another. The quickest way to 'cotton' low beds is to use a cottoning tool made by fixing a reel to the end of a stick about the size of a walking stick, with a large nail pushed through the middle of the reel. But all this takes time, and knowing from bitter experience that a new plantation of silvers must not be left unprotected for a single moment, I am gradually being converted to spraying the young plants with a weak mixture of Jeyes before I leave them. One teaspoonful to a gallon of water will not poison the birds, but must taste very nasty, for treated plants are left in peace until the Jeyes has been washed off, and by that time the bed has usually been accepted as part of the landscape.

CHAPTER 5

Pruning and Grooming

THE beauty and decorative value of silver-foliaged shrubs is probably more dependent on proper pruning and grooming than most other garden plants. Shapely specimens, densely covered with clean silver or white leaves are always worth a second glance, but there is nothing much more unsightly than an untidy mass of thin lustreless foliage. So it is essential to prune in such a way that there is always a continuity of young shoots waiting to take the place of those that have become tired and worn-out.

All silver- and grey-foliaged shrubs are fundamentally evergreen and continue growing throughout winter. Furthermore a cut at any time of year will encourage them to produce a number of young shoots. This habit is useful in spring and summer, but it does preclude autumn pruning, for sappy immature growth can never withstand frost. Hence the main pruning has to take place in spring. Hardy types such as *Santolina incana* or *Helichrysum splendidum* can be tackled in April, but May frosts are not uncommon and a newly trimmed *Artemisia arborescens* would have little chance of surviving the sort of May frost we get if it were not protected. Luckily late spring is the time when everything is in full growth, and shrubs that have been cut back in the middle of May are always well covered by early June.

Of course there is the occasional specimen standing in a prominent position which cannot be allowed to spoil the appearance of the whole garden and may have to be pruned and protected. Luckily spring frosts are of short duration, so the covering need not be elaborate. A sack or even a polythene bag will suffice provided it is slipped over the stump when frost is indicated and removed next morning.

Most varieties of silvers produce the best summer foliage when they are cut right back to within two nodes of the previous year's growth. This may seem drastic but it ensures sound development and an abundance of young shoots. As these shoots mature so they will tend to overcrowd and it is at this time that it is possible to pinch a few back to within one node and thus force through a later crop of shoots. It is this second layer which is needed to carry the plant through late summer when the early crop of foliage has become tatty.

However firmly one prunes it is impossible to prevent the formation of flowering growth. When this should be removed is a matter of choice. Very few shrubs with interesting leaves are blessed with interesting flowers and it is certainly difficult to get a shrub back into condition once it has started to make its seed. On the other hand some varieties are attractive when in bud, and the plants themselves can look somewhat bare if the flowering growth is cut away too soon before the second crop of shoots has had a chance to grow. Perhaps the right answer is to wait for the first flowers to show colour and then to get to work.

When dealing with Helichrysums, Senecios and Santolinas the entire flowering stem must be removed, for it comes straight from the heart of the shrub, and is quite capable of producing another flush of flowers if it is merely dead-headed. Growth that shows signs of elongating into bud or is thin and weak should be removed at the same time, so that the younger shoots can develop without risk of overcrowding.

The beauty of the late summer foliage of shrubs that have been groomed in this manner is worth the effort. Once the urge to flower has passed the leaves grow large and lustrous. Furthermore they remain spruce for a long time and it is not unusual for a pruned specimen to be as decorative in December as it was in June. So far as the health of the plants is concerned this routine will keep them compact and quite apart from appearance this is important, for untidy leads often get bruised by wind. On the whole silver-foliaged shrubs are immune from most of the diseases which plague most garden plants, but I have seen a fungoid rot enter a stem through a bruise and travel down towards the base.

It is unwise to cut or prune most silver-foliaged shrubs after the beginning of August. The last thing one wants in autumn is a crop of delicate young shoots and as the days shorten so it takes longer for the growth to mature.

Newly planted shrubs need special attention if they are to grow up into shapely specimens. Left to their own devices they tend to run to flower which can be disastrous and must be prevented at all costs. The ideal routine is to stop back each shoot in turn as soon as it is possible to nip it back to two nodes. This treatment, which must not be continued after the beginning of August, helps to promote a sound fibrous root system as well as a properly balanced top and is well worth while when the plants are intended to be grown as permanent features.

Herbaceous silvers require very little grooming, but as with most other perennials they are much more effective when their stems are given room to develop and do not become as overcrowded as they would be if every shoot were allowed to grow. Newly propagated plants seldom carry too many breaks, but when established plants are not going to be divided they must be thinned in spring. This serves not only to give the remaining shoots a better start but also encourages the formation of some very useful secondary growth.

Although the flowers of most silver perennials are not very exciting in themselves, their stems are usually well shaped and very heavily covered with felt, so that the general effect of the plants is very attractive when they are flowering. If the first stems are cut away as soon as they become untidy there should be a further display of flower in late summer.

Most gardeners cut back all their perennials when they tidy up their borders in autumn. This does not suit those with grey foliage, for they all have the tiresome habit of pushing their way through the ground in February. The old growth does afford some protection and when this has been removed the early shoots get badly frosted. This never hurts the plants themselves, but it delays the summer display and for this reason I would rather see everything tied up in autumn and cut back in March.

Although the natural instinct of grey-foliaged biennials is to come to flower and die during their second season, I prefer to think of them as monocarpic for they will live for so many years if not allowed to set seed. It is, of course, difficult to prevent seeding once the flowering spike has developed, but when plants are specifically grown for the sake of their magnificent leaves they can be kept going almost indefinitely.

Tall varieties, such as *Onopordon arabicum* and *Verbascum bombicyferum* are often needed as height at the back of the border, but can be quite infuriating when they decide to collapse in July and leave great gaps. This can be prevented by removing the flowering growth before it has had a chance to set seed. The main stem may well seem to be devoid of side-shoots, but it is amazing how quickly the breaks appear and elongate into branches once the lead has been removed. These secondaries never grow quite as tall as the main stem, but they flower well and make a good splash of colour. Subsequent dead-heading will encourage the formation of more breaks and thus prolong the life of the plant into late autumn.

A sharp eye has to be kept on plants that are being grown for foliage alone for the flowering spikes must be removed as soon as they appear so that they cannot rob the leaves. The main lead is always easy to find, but the side shoots which appear later are very cunning and try to hide themselves away behind large leaves. It does not take a second to cut away the little sprouts, but regular attention is essential, for the plants seem to know all about holidays and rush up to flower as soon as they think that they are going to be left in peace! Young flower spikes look rather like small rosettes on stalks, but in their earliest form merely consist of two small leaves growing out of a knobble. The leaves that matter look quite different when they are young, for they grow separately and always spring from the heart of the plant.

The one great failing of silver-foliaged plants of all descriptions is that they cling to their old leaves. This does not matter when the shrubs and perennials have been properly pruned and groomed, for the old foliage will either have been cut away before it withered or else tied up for the winter. With biennials however the removal of worn out leaves from the base of the plants is a small chore which should not be neglected, for these leaves are not only unsightly but can quite easily smother another plant in wet weather. Furthermore they harbour slugs, and there does not seem to be any kind of slug which does not delight in the fleshy roots and juicy leaves of these plants.

CHAPTER 6

Silvers in Urban Areas

EXPERTS may tell us that the air in urban areas is still heavily contaminated with petrol and diesel fumes, but there can be no question that the introduction of Clean Air Zones has made gardening much easier for some.

Silver-foliaged plants suffered badly in the days before the Act and could not be grown in London or in any other city. Even now, those who live anywhere near an industrial plant, such as the Battersea Power Station in London, find that their grey-leaved plants seldom remain healthy for any length of time. This is probably due to suffocation. Ordinary green leaves are smooth and can shed their grime, but when dirt falls on a rough surface it sticks, and no water or rain will wash it away. Before long such a thick layer of dirt has been built up on each leaf that the plant itself is no longer able to breathe.

How much damage is still being done to plants by petrol and diesel fumes is not really known, but it is noticeable that the very heavily felted shrubs, such as *Senecio cineraria*, cannot be relied on to overwinter when they are planted near main roads, while many others, including *Helichrysum fontanesii*, do not grow as freely in urban gardens as they do in the country.

That some deposit is still falling from the sky is shewn when soil tests are taken at intervals of a year, and most town dwellers find it essential to dress their borders annually with some form of living compost or fresh loam. Silvers are not particularly fussy, but their roots will shrivel when the soil becomes contaminated. It would, however, be extremely unwise to suggest any general panacea, for each area has its own particular problem and its own type of fall-out, and the local nurseryman is the one who has learnt how to tackle the trouble.

Lack of light is probably a worse enemy than pollution, for most town gardens are shady and most of their owners like to deceive themselves into imagining that they are sunny, even when they are actually only getting a couple of hours of sunlight. To get a good covering of felt or silk on to the leaves, silvers of all types need at least five hours of sunlight during the summer, and it is not really worth planting grey shrubs in positions which are shaded from the South and would not therefore get their fair share of light in winter.

Open positions are few and far between in urban gardens and, when there is a doubt about the light, it seems wiser to rely on perennials which do not resent winter shade in the same way. In the main these have silvery grey leaves, which means that a patch devoted to them is inclined to be dreary and needs highlighting with something brighter and more exciting. A clump of *Artemisia purshiana*, for example, is quite pretty but not exactly inspiring. The same clump though, will look very different when it is used as a background for a special white leaved specimen which might perhaps be either *Senecio cineraria* 'White Diamond', *Senecio leucostachys* or *Centaurea gymnocarpa* 'Colchester White'. Similarly, there is nothing very wonderful about the fern-like leaves of *Achillea* 'Moonshine' when seen by themselves, but they do show off the velvety texture of *Gazania* 'Silver Beauty' quite perfectly and gain in so doing. Even a clump of *Anaphalis triplinervis* is worth a second glance when it is surrounded by a mass of felty sprigs of *Helichrysum petiolatum*.

Gazania 'Silver Beauty', *Helichrysum petiolatum* and *Centaurea* 'Colchester White' are all tender varieties and neither of the Senecios mentioned could be guaranteed to overwinter in urban surroundings, so it may well seem that I am going back on my principles and advocating 'bedding-out'. To a limited extent this is so. Town gardeners have many problems to deal with and one of these is that their gardens are so small and compact that every part has to be kept well covered and tidy throughout the season. To achieve this some cheating must take place and 'bedding-out' is not really a crime. It is merely an extra chore and, as such, something to be avoided as far as possible. My suggestion is merely that just a few bold white-foliaged specimens be planted out annually amongst a groundwork of permanent residents and treated as expendable. This is not true 'bedding-out' but might be thought of as a form of additional embroidery!

When the position is really open, all the grey-foliaged shrubs such as Santolinas, Helichrysums and Artemisias are worth trying, but

Artemisia arborescens probably deserves a special mention, for records show that this was grown satisfactorily in London before the Clean Air Zones were even thought of. Usually growing to about three foot and well covered with feathery foliage, this is undoubtedly one of the most handsome of all the 'true' silver shrubs.

The Dwarf Achilleas *argentea* and P.D.166 are grey rather than white and therefore safe in 'clean' areas. *Antennaria aprica* and *A. dioica* are both useful little plants which cover the ground with a carpet of tiny rosettes. *Tanacetum densum amanum* is really too white, but *Leucanthemum hosmariensis* makes a pleasant little steely grey bush and often produces its marguerite-like flowers in winter as well as in spring and summer. *Anthemis rudolphiana* is one of the tidiest plants I know and always grows into a perfectly circular cushion of deeply cut lacy leaves. *Artemisia lanata pedemontana* is more of a carpeting plant. It is semi-shrubby and keeps its bright silky foliage throughout most of the year. *Artemisia schmidtiana*, on the other hand, is herbaceous and not so silvery, but it has – like *Artemisia arborescens* – a very fine record of survival in polluted areas, and the cushions of silky foliage it forms are extremely decorative. In certain years, the whole of the cushion turns bright russet in autumn and remains so for two or more weeks before the plant finally decides to hibernate.

The foliage of certain hybrid pinks is so tidy and so good in winter that they would deserve a place in any garden, even if they did not flower. Probably the best of all for foliage effect is 'Pink Bouquet' which makes tight mounds of pale grey-blue and has sugar pink flowers. The habit of 'Anthony' is similar but the foliage is a little darker and the flower claret-coloured. These two cultivars cover about a foot of space in their first year. On a smaller scale, there are 'Crimson Treasure' and 'Rose Treasure', both of which manage to look fresh and clean on the very worst day of winter and yet are seldom found without a flower in summer.

Provided the positions chosen are reasonably sunny, many types of grey-foliaged plants can be grown either in window boxes or in tubs and troughs on roof gardens, and because they do not object to wind are often the best choice for draughty sites. This is, perhaps, not as strange as it may sound, for there is some similarity between the wall of a house and the side of a cliff, and when a plant has been equipped by nature to withstand the kind of gusty breezes associated with hilly country, it should be capable of taking a few draughts in its stride.

The boxes and troughs used for grey foliaged plants need to be well drained and must have at least an inch of broken crocks spread over the bottom. Some modern boxes are sold without drainage holes, and though this idea may suit other things, it does not agree with silvers. One hole is sufficient, provided the crocks are so placed that it is protected and cannot get blocked by wandering roots.

The most satisfactory medium for window boxes and troughs is a soil compost made up to the J.I. No. 1 standard. The nutrients in this mixture are perfectly balanced and should give everything a good start. There is a danger, however, that in hot summers the plants will exhaust their supply of nitrogen. Early signs of nitrogen deficiency usually show up towards the end of July and include thin top growth and a yellowing of the lower leaves. This can be prevented if each plant is given a teaspoonful of dried blood during prolonged periods of bright sunny weather. The blood is scattered round the plants after they have been watered and must be washed down into the roots with a little more water.

With window boxes it is all too easy to wash all the nutrients out of the soil by giving the plants an unnecessary amount of water, but sufficient must be given to ensure that it reaches down to the roots. By wetting the top surface ten minutes before watering it is easy to judge how much needs to be given so that the plants get a proper drink without the box being flooded. Some watering and subsequent loss of food can be prevented if the surface of the compost is mulched with half an inch of chippings, gravel or even pebbles.

Even the very best top-spit loam loses its life after twelve months in a box, and there is no known formula which will produce a compost capable of sustaining good growth after the first year. Ideally, all window boxes and troughs should be emptied and scrubbed out each year, but when the box still contains sound plants it is easier to scrape away as much of the old soil as possible with a table fork and introduce fresh soil. Experiments suggest that it is better to use a J.I. No. 2 mix for older plants.

Most window boxes are shallow and narrow and those who have never had anything to do with them are inclined to be far too optimistic and to expect the plants they use to last for ever! In my experience there are no silvers which will do more than give two good seasons, for those that are capable of making a show in their first year are too vigorous and would smother the entire window if left for a third year, while the slower types would be too small and insignificant in their first season.

The best immediate effects are undoubtedly achieved by planting two year old specimens of varieties which can be kept to size by pruning. Even a vigorous plant such as *Senecio laxifolius* can be shaped and kept as a tidy little eighteen-inch bush for at least a couple of years, if its lanky leads are either shortened or cut away whenever they show signs of getting out of hand. The art of this sort of pruning is to spread it out and never to attack too many leads at a time. Regular snipping will keep the plant compact and prevent gaps developing and, when well done, should result in a neat bush well covered at all times with clean young shoots.

Senecio cineraria 'White Diamond' responds well to this sort of treatment, but, being comparatively slow growing, does not require such frequent trimming as *S. laxifolius*. It is an impressive plant and most attractive when its bold white leaves can be contrasted with the needle-like silvery foliage of *Helichrysum angustifolium* and the flowing felty sprays of *Helichrysum petiolatum*. This is my favourite selection for a window, for *Helichrysum angustifolium* can be kept as a formal bush by clipping, while *H. petiolatum* needs no encouragement to help it to flow gracefully over the front edge of the box.

A window box filled with just one subject would be very dull and there is usually enough room for at least three different types. To get a good effect from a distance there must be some contrasts, not only of shape, but also of texture. A good and easy association is that of *Artemisia splendens*, *Helichrysum plicatum* and *Artemisia stelleriana*. *A. splendens* is a very lovely tufted perennial which will grow into a low clump of misty grey if its main lead is shortened back. The cloud-like impression given by this plant is always enhanced when it is stood against something rather solid like *Helichrysum plicatum*. This has narrow, pale grey leaves which, in turn, benefit from the contrast with the bold chrysanthemum-like foliage of *Artemisia stelleriana*.

There are many possibilities and a number of plants to choose from, but *Santolina neapolitana* and *serratifolia* are best avoided for they would need constant pruning to keep them to size and their young shoots remain green for several weeks. This does not apply to the ordinary Lavender Cotton, *Santolina chamaecyparisus* (*S. incana*) nor to its cultivar 'Weston' which is a woolly treasure, but probably too slow for most window boxes.

The deep troughs that are usually used on roof gardens are ideally suited for silvers and there is generally just enough space available to enable a few shrubs to be grown into reasonably sized specimens. All the shrubs mentioned so far for both town gardens and window boxes would flourish on a roof, but it would not be very satisfactory to try any of the herbaceous plants such as *Artemisia purshiana*, for their roots would not take kindly to confinement! When there is a wall to be covered, *Teucrium fruticans* is invaluable for it will spread out over three feet in a year when young, but can be kept to four feet if need be. The stems of *fruticans* are white and the leaves silver. It is a decorative plant at all times of year and very beautiful in May when it smothers itself with pale lilac bracts. Although it grows so freely, it is not a greedy variety and is quite content to remain for years in an 18″ tub, if the soil is renewed annually.

There is often a place for a box containing small treasures on a roof and this might be a good position for the most attractive of all the Santolinas, *S. chamaecyparissus* c. Weston, which is so much whiter than the ordinary Lavender Cotton and never grows to much more than nine inches. Of course, all the Achilleas, Antennarias and Artemisias, and the 'Treasure Pinks' mentioned earlier, would be just as happy on a roof as they would on the ground, but mention should be made here of *Artemisia glacialis* which is really a smaller version of *A. lanata pedemontana*. If a superb small shrub is needed, nothing could be better or more desirable than *Convolvulus cneorum*. This gem covers itself with white flowers in late spring, but it is the lustre of its leaves which is so exciting, for in bright weather they shine like well polished cutlery. It is not the easiest plant to grow but there are several good specimens to be found in London, and the best of these are all growing in roof gardens.

CHAPTER 7

Under Glass

SILVERS can be very tricky under glass. It is not that the plants themselves are so difficult to grow, but rather that the foliage is inclined to remain green when conditions are not perfect. This can be heart-breaking, for there is nothing much more depressing than the jaundiced appearance of grey- or white-foliaged plants when their leaves have refused to produce a proper covering.

Full light and a buoyant atmosphere are essential and this makes it almost impossible to mix silvers with most other ornamental foliages. They are, however, perfectly happy in carnation houses and often do well in conservatories and hot dry sun-parlours where it is difficult to grow anything but cacti. A light shading in summer is not really essential but will do no harm if it is not put on too heavily and is cleared away early in August.

Very little heat is required and, provided the frost is kept at bay, it is better to keep the temperature on the cool side in the depth of winter. Young growth stimulated by heat during the dark months is always soft and sappy and never grows a good crop of hair! From mid-February onwards the sun starts to gather strength and then the heat can be raised slightly after clear bright days, though it is never safe to let the temperature rise much above 50 degrees Fahrenheit at night.

The production of hairs and felt on the leaves would also seem to be affected by the amount of nutrients in the potting compost. When this is on the rich side and the plants are able to stuff themselves the leaves become coarse and insist on remaining bald. A weak mixture, such as a J.I. No. 1 would therefore seem the right choice, but unfortunately all plants absorb a lot of nitrogen in hot sunny weather and this may have to be replaced by feeding with light dressings of dried blood. A teaspoonful per plant is usually sufficient to replace the nitrogen used by a young plant in a 4½″ pot during fourteen bright days in June or July, but older and larger specimens may need a double dose. Dried blood is one of the safest of all the nitrogenous feeds, but can burn the roots of dry plants. For this reason they must be well watered before feeding and the feed must be carefully washed down into the compost.

Although many glasshouses and sun-parlours have beds, silvers under glass seem happier when they are in pots and it is a fact that the foliage seems to turn silver much quicker when the plants are very slightly pot-bound. Most varieties can be kept in either 5″ or 6″ clay pots until their third year when they will need a 7½″ or 8″ pot. Alpines always do best in shallow pans. Very few are capable of covering a 6″ pan in a year, but if three are planted together they will grow into one another and make a brave show within a few weeks.

Many growers, when they are potting, insist on using a rammer to consolidate the soil, regardless of the type of plant they are dealing with. This is fatal with grey-foliaged varieties for their roots are not capable of working their way into a hard packed mass of soil. Loose potting would, of course, be equally unsuitable but, as in all things, there is a mean, and it is possible to avoid air pockets and make the compost reasonably solid by thumping the base of the pot on the bench and finishing off the sides with finger pressure. Sufficient room for water must always be left clear. Half an inch between soil level and rim is sufficient for 5″ pots but larger sizes need at least an inch.

Good specimens of most silvers can be kept growing for many a year if they are given a change of soil biennially, but the job must be done both carefully and thoroughly, for though as much as possible of the old soil must be removed, care must be taken not to damage the main roots. The best method is to tip the plant out of the pot and let both crocks and compost fall away, but this will not happen if the plant has just been watered. It is of course advisable to re-pot into clean pots with clean crocks.

Re-potting can be undertaken either in September or March. September is probably best when a display is wanted for spring or early summer, though certain varieties can be kept in condition from July to February if they are dealt with in March.

For the sake of convenience the main annual pruning is best done just before re-potting. Nearly all grey-foliaged plants can take drastic pruning if needs be but it is only really necessary to cut away all weak stems and shorten back the current year's wood to two nodes. Pruning should produce quantities of shoots, some of which can be stopped while still young in order to ensure a continuity of good foliage.

All pot plants need sufficient air space in which to develop, especially if they are to grow into shapely specimens, well 'feathered' from the base upwards. Overcrowding kills off all the lower leaves and shoots and encourages too much thin top growth. Regular turning is also important when shape matters and this is a very good reason for keeping the plants in pots. Silvers are sun-lovers and will always try to face the sun. By giving the plants a twist every week all four sides can be made to develop simultaneously.

Opinions vary as to the best material on which to stand the pots. Bare earth and peat would both be unsuitable for they would encourage worms, and the roots which did happen to wander into the soil would certainly get broken every time the plants were moved. A base of cinders is quite good provided the cinders have been well weathered, but I am sure that there is nothing to beat a 3″ layer of gravel, with sand as a second choice. In summer extra gravel or sand can be worked in amongst the pots. This saves a lot of watering but does nothing for the roots in winter when they must be allowed to dry out quickly after watering.

How often to water silvers is largely a matter of experience and of observation. Water must certainly never be given when it is not required, but equally the plants should not be allowed to dry out, for when this happens the foliage loses its lustre. In the dark days of winter very little water is needed but when the surge of growth becomes evident in April, the plants may well need watering every day. Skilled plantsmen can tell the exact condition of the soil by knocking the pots with a hammer, but those who do not trust their ears can get a pretty good idea by examining the tips of the upper leaves as these lose their resilience and become slightly flabby when the roots start to feel dry. This must be done either in the morning or when the sun has gone off the glass in the evening for the top growth of most plants tends to flag during the heat of the day and this could easily be taken as a sign of dry roots. A serious surfeit of water will also lead to flagging, but in this case it is not only the top growth which droops but rather the whole plant, including the leaves at the base.

Watering has always been looked on as a skilled job and it is certainly none too easy to water pots that have been allowed to get fairly dry. There is always the risk that the water given may not reach the roots, or, alternatively, that all the nutrients may be washed out of the soil. If the plants have been correctly potted it should be sufficient to fill the space between the compost and the rim of the pot with water if the surface has been wetted a few minutes ahead of watering. Sometimes, when the plants have been allowed to dry out, bubbles will keep on gurgling away while the water is draining down and, when this happens, it is better to drop the pot into a bucket containing three inches of water so that it can suck up what it needs by capillary action. When watering in summer it is always a good idea to wet the bed on which the pots are standing. This cools the roots and prevents the compost at the bottom of the pots from getting too dry.

Sometimes a wretched worm wanders up into a pot and manages to block the drainage hole. Worms are invaluable creatures and normally should be treated as friends, but there is a place for everything and a pot containing a silver plant is not the right place for a worm. Luckily a fault in the drainage can be spotted pretty well immediately for the water just stays on the surface and does not try to run down into the compost. When this happens the pot must be turned on to its side quickly so as to get rid of the water, otherwise the plant would immediately start to droop and might well be dead within an hour. There is no cure except re-potting and it is not enough just to remove the worm which will have dragged the compost down into the crocks.

When height is needed for the wall of a conservatory or sun-parlour, one of the most useful varieties is *Teucrium fruticans* which, when tied to a trellis, is capable of covering a large surface in a very short time and can stand a lot of heat in summer. This is one variety which does need a large container, for it would be a tedious business to untie every lead each autumn in order to re-pot the root. Good specimens can be grown and kept for many years in an 18″ tub if the top five inches of soil is changed annually. Under glass, *Teucrium fruticans* finds it hard to decide when to flower, but usually manages at least three crops in a year. Even if it did not flower, it would still be worth growing for the sake of its white stems and bright silver leaves, but the lavender blue flowers, which are produced in profusion, are a very pleasant bonus. This shrub can be kept going nicely if it is merely dead-headed, but should more drastic pruning be necessary, it is probably best done in September after the autumn flowering.

Teucrium fruticans azurea is not so well known. It is small and slow, but well worth growing for the sake of its delicate white foliage and true-blue flowers. Young plants are not impressive and take about three years to reach their full potential.

Helichrysum petiolatum is usually seen as a procumbent plant spreading a mass of lovely pale grey 'arms' over the surrounding ground, but it is not always realised how magnificent it can be when trained against a wall. Plants intended for this sort of treatment must be tied to a stake as soon as they are planted and may need one or two further ties as they grow. Once their side shoots have reached the trellis, however, they only need threading through the splines. A good specimen can be kept for many years if potted into a tub like *Teucrium fruticans*, but may overgrow its space if not cut back drastically every spring. When smaller specimens are needed for the front of the bench, they can be potted into quite small pots for their roots are thread-like and do not take up much space. The flowers are poor and carried on bare stems. These stems are easy to spot, and will not develop if the plants are kept in condition by regular 'nipping'. *Helichrysum petiolatum* is a plant that can be lifted at any time, however large it may be, and if outdoor specimens are brought under cover in September they often remain decorative throughout the winter. The trick is to prepare the roots at least a week before lifting. In dry weather this may involve watering as well as cutting round the root with a spade or fork. The roots are not very good at holding on to their soil and usually come out of the ground looking practically naked. This does not seem to worry the plants for if they are popped into pots straight away and given a drink, none of the foliage suffers! If only wanted for winter decoration no special compost is needed and the garden soil from which they were taken should be adequate.

Several different Centaureas can be grown under glass, but *C. gymnocarpa* 'Colchester White' seems to be the most useful, for its deeply cut long drooping leaves are quite distinct and the plant retains its white appearance, even after flowering. The mauve flowers are thistle-like and come on white stems. Whether they are worth keeping is a matter of opinion, but they are certainly not without charm. Heavy pruning is inadvisable for this is a variety which seldom breaks from the base, and its instinct is to grow into a somewhat palm-like standard. The total removal of all flowering growth is, however, essential, for if a little piece of a stem is left, it will immediately make a further attempt to flower.

The formation of the white leaves of *Chrysanthemum ptarmacaefolium* is fascinating to study and could be said to remind one of a superb example of fine lace work. Often used as a bedding plant, this shrub is slow growing and only shows its true beauty in its second year. It has no particular foibles except an intense dislike of frost, and responds well to being pruned in March.

Velvet is a word often used in connection with certain grey-foliaged plants but it should really be reserved to describe the leaves of *Sideritis candicans*, for they really do look as though they had been stamped out of a length of the most superb soft grey velvet. A tender shrub, best pruned in March, this variety can be kept looking well throughout the year if it is stopped regularly.

Convolvulus cneorum is another treasure which can be grown in a pot. In the garden its silvery leaves often get marked, but under glass every silky hair reflects the light and the whole plant shimmers when the sun is shining. It usually starts flowering in March but often gives two repeat performances, the first in July and the last in October. The individual flowers are somewhat like those of the common bindweed, but they come in clusters and open in turn. Thus the flowering period often lasts for more than a month. *Convolvulus cneorum* is a slow grower and needs little pruning, but if a plant should become too big for its position it can be cut back. Re-potting is best done in September.

Although virtually hardy, *Senecio cineraria* 'White Diamond' is such a good plant and has such bold white leaves that it deserves a place of honour in any sun-parlour or conservatory. The only snag with this variety is that it always gets an urge to flower in summer. This can be infuriating for, once the stems start to elongate into bud, the lustre goes from the leaves and the plants lose all their beauty. Mere dead-heading is useless under glass and the whole of the limb must be cut right out. There should be a second layer of foliage ready if every second shoot which appears after pruning is stopped when about four inches long but it will, of course, be somewhat green through lack of light and may take a fortnight or so before it has developed any felt. Incidentally, the flower, which is the cause of all this trouble, is certainly not worth keeping, being more like an untidy dandelion than anything else. Senecios can be potted and pruned either in September or March, September being best for early summer display. March plants only reach their zenith in July, which is well past the natural flowering season, and in certain years, when the skies are overcast, they make no attempt to 'run' and stay in perfect condition for a further six months. When, however, the weather is hot in July, the tell-tale signs show up very quickly: the leaves become thin and pointed and flowering stems start to emerge. If these stems are cut back straight away, the second crop of foliage should mature within a couple of weeks and nothing is lost.

Although 'White Diamond' is the whitest and most shapely of all the *Senecio cineraria* cultivars its foliage is not particularly easy to harden, and those who use their indoor plants for cutting would be well advised to choose 'Ramparts' instead. This is a much more vigorous plant and has a tendency to grow rather tall if its shoots are not nipped back as they develop. Incidentally, this treatment encourages the leaves to spread, which makes them much more useful for arranging.

When the foliage is finely cut and really white, *Senecio leucostachys* is a delightful plant to own, but it sometimes goes mad and produces a mass of coarse dirty-green growth. This can be the result of over-feeding, or more often of over-watering combined with a lack of light, and it is certainly a variety which needs to be kept fairly dry at all times and very dry in early spring. If 'rogue' growth does appear, the only cure is to cut it back and hope that, by keeping the plant dry, the next crop will come white. The clusters of cream coloured flowers of this Senecio are quite attractive and they do not seem to damage the foliage in any way, provided they are not allowed to go to seed. Once they are cut down, bunches of little white shoots appear within a week and these are sufficiently decorative to keep the plant well clothed until late autumn. The most attractive specimens are those potted and pruned in September and partially stopped in March. *Senecio leucostachys* is a very brittle plant which can easily lose an entire side if a shoot is mishandled. For this reason only, it is advisable to put a loose tie round the shoots while they are still young and pliable.

Foliage taken from indoor specimens of *Senecio laxifolius* is very different from that cut from the open border, each leaf being perfectly formed and heavily outlined with white. Furthermore, this shrub can grow into some very decorative shapes under glass which makes it well worth while for those looking for artistic effect rather than botanical interest. How much to prune is a matter of choice. It will, of course, stand any amount of cutting at any time, but when pruned severely develops into a round bush, which may not be what is wanted! Thinning the shoots is probably as important as pruning, for the beauty of the individual leaves cannot be appreciated if they are crushed together by overcrowding.

When a carpet is needed for the front of a bench or border, there is nothing to rival a mixture of *Helichrysum petiolatum* and *Gazania* 'Silver Beauty'. I have already extolled the beauty of the Helichrysum as a wall plant, but it is just as lovely when seen spreading its long 'arms' towards a bold clump of 'Silver Beauty'. This plant, which is a hybrid of unknown origin, has probably the most densely felted foliage of all the Gazania cultivars, and it is seldom that one can find even one young leaf that is not properly covered with white hairs. The flowers, which close in the afternoon, are bright yellow with a black eye. Flowering does not seem to overtax the strength of the plant and certainly does not rob any of the leaves of their intrinsic beauty. If *Gazania* 'Silver Beauty' has a failing, it is that it grows too well and covers too much space. As this applies equally to the Helichrysum it would be unwise to plant them at less than 14″ and even so, they may need tidying back in summer. Both varieties are perennial and can be kept and re-potted in September, but it is probably easier to replant each year with cuttings rooted in February.

Aromatic foliage is always pleasant and there can be few leaves that smell more delicious than those of *Lavendula lanata*. This is the white-foliaged lavender of Spain which is not a particularly easy herb to cultivate in the open. Under glass, however, it is a good, if slow growing, pot plant, which only needs full sun and a dry atmosphere in winter. The dark blue flowers are a little disappointing for they have not got as much scent as the heavily felted leaves.

Two Artemisias are strongly aromatic and, though not particularly outstanding in appearance, are good to rub against. The first is the Sage Bush of America, *Artemisia tridentata* and the second *Artemisia nutans*, a Sicilian perennial. Both are easy and respond best to being pruned and potted in September.

Some may like the smell given off by *Helichrysum angustifolium*, but those who dislike curry would be well advised not to allow a plant anywhere near their glasshouses, for the smell is pervading. Nevertheless *H. angustifolium* is good under glass for it keeps silver throughout the year with the very minimum of trouble and can be very decorative. Drastic pruning is seldom required if all flowering growth and lanky stems are clipped back as they develop.

Experimenting with the ordinary garden silvers under glass can be very rewarding for there is always a chance that the foliage may be just that bit more exciting when it has not been marked and bruised by wind and rain. *Artemisia arborescens*, for example, responds magnificently to glasshouse culture and the foliage of covered specimens has an ethereal quality seldom seen in the garden. Sometimes though, the experiments may be just as disappointing, for there are varieties that need the drying effect of the wind and will not turn grey without it. Thus it seems impossible to get a proper silver sheen on to *Artemisia schmidtiana*, however carefully it may be grown.

Even under glass, silvers are seldom worried by either insects or disease. Just occasionally there may be an odd cluster of greenfly to be found nestling round a flowering stem or in the heart of a young shoot, but all kinds of fly can be killed quickly with a spray of nicotine, or of any other suitable proprietary greenfly cure that does not contain a soapy emulsion. If leaf miner does get a hold, it can be more serious as the only chemical cure seems to be Lindex Miscible and this makes a sorry mess of the foliage which does not clear up for a week or so. Heavy infestations can, however, be avoided if all the plants are carefully examined the moment the first sign of trouble is seen, and if every dubious leaf is removed and burnt.

The only disease normally seen is grey mould or botrytis and this only appears when frost has been able to get into the house or when the atmosphere has been allowed to get too damp. Spraying with Orthocide will control the fungus but care must be taken to see that the air is kept moving after an attack.

Many house-plant enthusiasts have learnt that though grey-foliaged plants cannot be grown in the house, some can be brought into a living room and kept happy for several weeks. How long they can stay is entirely dependent on the condition of the young leaves when the plant is brought in. If they have a good cover of felt or silk, the plant will remain attractive for quite a while, for the leaf covering does not fade away even when deprived of light. It must be remembered though, that the plants themselves will continue to grow and that, in their efforts to find the light, their stems will lengthen and 'draw'. In addition, all the new leaves produced in the dark of the living room are bound to remain naked and green. Thus the appearance of any silver must deteriorate if it is left indoors for any length of time. The plants can be helped to a limited extent if they are stood in a South-facing window and turned daily. Another trick is to stand the whole pot out in the sun on bright days. I did once manage to keep a large specimen of *Helichrysum petiolatum* which had been dug out of the border in September, till after Christmas, but I have never yet been able to keep a plant of *Senecio cineraria* 'White Diamond' in a sitting room for more than six weeks.

Sideritis candicans is perhaps the one exception. Well grown plants, cut back in June and brought into the house in October, do not put on much growth during the winter months and retain their velvety appearance till spring, even if they are not stood in the full light. They look so well, in fact, that it is only when one comes to examine the foliage carefully that one realises that the leaves have turned yellow under the heavy layer of silky fibre and that the time has come to allow the poor plants a long period of convalescence.

CHAPTER 8

Decorative Material

MOST flower decorators have learnt, through bitter experience, that though it is quite easy to make interesting arrangements with shop flowers, foliage bought from the florist is seldom satisfactory. There is, in any case, remarkably little choice, and when it comes to silver or grey material one seldom finds anything but Eucalyptus.

Luckily, a good supply of grey foliage can be grown without very much trouble if a small area is set aside for the purpose. Some bits and pieces can, of course, be taken from the border, but most of the stems will be straight if the plants have been groomed, and it is a lot easier to achieve exciting designs when one starts with a few natural curves. Furthermore, too much cutting does not improve the look of any border.

There is also the question of continuity. The average border planned for decorative effect will not produce much grey cutting material from September onwards. By then most of the shrubs are taboo and it is hard to find good pieces on perennials when they are coming to the end of their season.

Cutting borders are therefore a necessity for the enthusiastic arranger but these must be carefully planned so that the material they yield is properly balanced and available for as long a season as possible. Two distinct types of foliage are needed: branches and stems to use as framework or outline, and shapely leaves of varying sizes to give body to designs.

Obviously the choice of varieties must be dependent on the kind of work the material is needed for, but I would have thought that every decorator needed at least one plant of *Senecio laxifolius* (or the hardy form of *S. greyii*) and probably several more. Throughout most of the country this is a reasonably hardy plant providing its roots are standing on good drainage, and it does not seem to suffer any damage if a few sprigs are removed in autumn or even in winter. The individual leaves are grey, clearly outlined with white, and one can usually find a good variety of different shaped pieces which can be used either as 'outline' or as 'body'. As a bonus there are the white stems in summer. These are at their best when cut before the buds open. *Senecio laxifolius* is a 'Cut and Come Again' shrub, capable of replacing itself throughout the growing season. When grown for cut it is best left unpruned in spring so that each piece can be taken with a bit of old wood attached. This not only facilitates hardening, but also makes it possible to find pieces suitable for three-foot arrangements.

Santolinas can also be cut in late summer, autumn and winter though it would be very unwise to cut so much away that the stumps were left bare! *S. neapolitana* and its variety *serratifolia* have identical feathery foliage which improves after it has been in water for a while. Stems vary in length from a foot to eighteen inches.

Established plants of *Ballota pseudodictamnus* are particularly prolific, and though the lower leaves may be apple green rather than grey, the tips of each stem might well be cut out of white velvet. If long stalks are wanted the plants must be pruned in April. The mauve flowers of this variety are inconspicuous but have apple green calyces. These grow in whorls round the stems which can be cut as soon as six whorls have formed. At this stage they should harden sufficiently for use in the house, but there is a danger that the growth may not yet be sufficiently mature to stand the heat of a tent on a hot day and for show work I prefer to use stems that are showing a few mauve flowers at the base. When there is any doubt about the maturity of the stem it is better to remove the soft top, nipping it back into the top whorl. If this is done neatly it should not show and the result is quite attractive. The first crop should start in June. This is followed by a second crop in August which carries on into October. Clusters of young shoots are very tempting but bleed and wilt quickly in water unless they are taken with a few inches of wood.

In summer the herbaceous Artemisias come into their own. Their only fault is that they grow too willingly and tend to throttle all their neighbours, but they certainly earn their keep. In early summer their stems are difficult to condition until they have become slightly woody, and it is asking for trouble to cut into the sappy growth when arranging. As the season goes on, however, all the stems lose their sappiness and become much easier to handle. The individual flowers are minute and borne in racemes forming spiky panicles. Although lacy in texture, these panicles tend to be too clumsy in shape for some outlines and are often improved by thinning. Flowering stems can be dried but do not keep as bright a silver as those cut from *Artemisia nutans*.

When the little flowers of *Artemisia* 'Lambrook Silver' open they look somewhat like the bobbles of Mimosa, but I doubt whether this variety would warrant a place in a cutting border were it not for the value of the large carrot-shaped leaves found at the base of the flowering stems in late summer and autumn. These are a good grey and, because they grow on five-inch stems, can easily be encouraged to flow over the front of the container.

Some of the shrubby Helichrysums such as *fontanesii* and *plicatum* can be persuaded to produce 18" long stems if their side shoots are removed as they develop. The long thin white leaves of these varieties make them particularly suitable for using with carnations. The other Helichrysum which is worth growing for cut is *H. petiolatum*. Although not hardy, it grows at such a rate that plants set out in May will yield an abundance of graceful curving leads from August onwards. I have cut it after a ten degree frost but usually lose it when the thermometer goes below twenty degrees Fahrenheit.

Senecio leucostachys is certainly hardier than *Helichrysum petiolatum* and can be overwintered on light land, but it is a comparatively slow grower and will not make much cuttable material in its first year. It is, however, a very worthwhile variety for the decorator, for when a lacy texture is required, there is nothing else which can provide such white sprigs. Immature shoots are green and will not take water, but once these have felted over they are easy to harden and will last for many weeks on end. The stems, however, become extremely brittle as the growth matures and, if curves are wanted, the shoots must be trained while they are still soft and green.

Home grown branches of Eucalyptus are extremely decorative and I would suggest that anyone who has a fairly warm garden and who needs a lot of decorative material should at least try growing *Eucalyptus gunnii*. It is unwise to rely entirely on a specimen planted for garden effect. This is a tree which is largely dependent on its beauty of shape and heavy cutting would probably unbalance it. Furthermore, the leaves on the upper branches of established trees are always pointed rather than rounded and therefore not nearly so decorative. When Eucalyps are grown specifically for cutting and their trunks are kept to about three feet, they will produce a very reasonable quantity of branches composed mainly of 'juvenile' leaves for some years. This sort of foliage is easy to harden and keeps for several weeks, but it is as well to remember that the branches are capable of drinking an abnormal amount of water when cut and that they can empty a container quicker than any other form of living material I know!

For really large work there is nothing in the grey line to compare with a mixture of *Verbascum bombicyferum* and *Onopordon arabicum*. It is true that six-foot designs can only be achieved in the height of summer, but it is surprising what large arrangements can be put together out of the side shoots of these two varieties in autumn if the plants have been carefully tended and not allowed to seed.

Sowing a few seeds of these two varieties at intervals throughout spring and summer ensures an invaluable supply of large leaves. Both kinds are useful for giving body to medium and large arrangements but it is the architectural beauty of the leaves of *Onopordon arabicum* which attracts the most attention, for they are so superbly sculptured that they can stand on their own. Incidentally, it is not merely this generation which appreciates the form of these particular leaves, as those who have studied Jacobean embroidery will no doubt have noticed.

Many other varieties have the sort of grey leaves needed for emphasising the heart of designs. In small and medium sized work those of the Horned Poppies, *Glaucium flavum* and *Glaucium corniculatum* can be used in much the same way as those of the Onopordon for they are beautifully made, stand on three-inch stems and look attractive from all angles. The plants, being monocarpic, grow fast but collapse as soon as they set seed. However, they are capable of throwing all their energy into making leaves as soon as their flowering stems are removed and it is possible to cut a lot from each plant. The only snag with these poppies is that their leaves are extremely brittle and have to be handled with care.

Some years ago I saw an arrangement of Gloxinias standing against a cluster of lovely woolly *Salvia argentea* leaves. I am not particularly fond of Gloxinias, but this was a memorable association. Since then I have learnt that there is something about the leaves of *Salvia argentea* which focuses attention on to the texture of most flowers. They are not easy to position because they can seldom be cut with stems more than two inches long, but they have a certain exotic quality and are capable of transforming a very humble bunch of flowers into something rich and rare. *Salvia argentea* leaves will harden when they are at their woolliest providing they have been exposed to the full rays of the sun and have not been partly covered with old foliage. Young flowering spikes, whilst still at the rosette stage, can also be used. These have slightly longer stalks than the leaves.

Although the flowering stems of *Stachys lanata* are inclined to be heavy and can be very irritating when their tips insist on following the light, their leaves are good for filling out the base of small arrangements and can be placed so as to form a design within a design. The non-flowering type known as 'Silver Carpet' is not so woolly and certainly not as interesting in early summer, but it keeps in good condition and comes into its own in July when the leaves of *S. lanata* are getting somewhat weather-worn.

Foliage cut from *Senecio cineraria* seedlings is unreliable and often wilts for no apparent reason. Much the same applies to anything cut from 'White Diamond' or 'Alice', but not, for some unknown reason, to pieces taken from 'Ramparts' which will often last for a month if properly conditioned. The leaves of this cultivar are large and the shoots somewhat clumsy, but if the lower leaves are removed and used at the base of the design it is sometimes possible to bring the tip and top leaf up on to the outline. When material is wanted for small work it is unnecessarily extravagant to cut a whole shoot as single leaves condition just as well as stems.

None of the various kinds of grey leaves can be conditioned by floating in water, which is inclined to mat the hairs of the felted subjects and wash the bloom off glaucous material. Hardening techniques vary, some varieties requiring the hot water treatment and others a quick singe. This is dealt with in detail, together with descriptions and advice on the growing of the better varieties, at the end of the book. Certain principles, however, apply to all grey material.

The first is the necessity of selecting pieces capable of taking up water, for it is always chancy to try to harden a soft sappy stem. In most varieties 'felting' increases as the shoots mature, so it might be said that the whiter the piece the more likely it is to keep. In early summer it is always more difficult to condition grey foliage cut in wet weather than it is during a drought, and pieces taken from plants grown on wet land will never respond as well as those cut from a dry plot. Leaves brought indoors while still wet seldom regain their clean appearance unless they are deliberately dried off with a cold blast from a hair drier, which disentangles the fibres.

It is always safer to cut any silver foliage needed for special occasions at least a day before it is required. It is the first six hours which matter and once the leaves have survived this period they should keep perfectly well for several days.

Cut surfaces dry out far quicker than most people realise and perhaps the real secret of keeping foliage is not to allow it to wilt in the first ten minutes. It is vital that there be no time-lag between cutting and getting the stems into water. I always take a bucket containing three inches of water to the plants and pop each piece into it as it is cut, rather than waiting to collect a complete bunch. Even when a variety needs singeing, each piece should be dealt with in turn in the garden and put straight into the bucket. Incidentally, it is not necessary to frizzle up the base of the stems and a cigarette lighter is quite adequate for the job.

Three inches of water is not, of course, sufficient to harden anything over a foot in length, but it is light to carry and does not make a nasty mess of the lower leaves which have to be removed before the foliage goes into the proper hardening bucket. Rotting leaves contaminate and thicken the water; this in turn, clogs the stems and very often accounts for the collapse not only of the foliage but also of the flowers with which it may eventually be used.

When hot water is used for hard wood, such as that of *Senecio laxifolius*, it needs to be very hot indeed and the steam produced can damage the foliage if it is allowed to rise. This can be prevented if the hardening is done in a fairly narrow necked jar wedged with a piece of newspaper to prevent the escape of steam.

Very short-stemmed leaves are tricky, for if the vein at the back of a furry leaf becomes sodden it cannot be dried out and will eventually siphon all the water out of a container on to the table. I keep a collection of potted meat jars for this purpose and stand the leaves upright in these, making sure that the water covers the base of the stems but does not reach the leaves themselves. When travelling, the necks of the jars have to be wedged with something to prevent splashing.

However carefully foliage is hardened, all the good work will be wasted if it is left scattered over the bench when the design is being put together. This is fatally easy to do. One picks up a piece, looks at it and then decides that it is not right. Meanwhile, the perfectly shaped stem has appeared and the first piece is forgotten. At home, a nice large bowl filled with chicken wire and just a little water is invaluable for holding rejected pieces. At a Show this would be something else to carry, but one can have a small jar filled with water and train oneself never to throw anything on to the table just because it is wrong for a certain position. Good foliage does not fall like Manna from Heaven. It has to be grown, cut and conditioned and deserves cherishing.

In the home, properly prepared silver foliage will outlast most flowers and can often be used more than once. No living material is ever really happy in a very dry atmosphere, but an all-grey design can be kept going for a considerable time in a centrally heated room if the level of the water is kept constant and the container is stood on something damp at night. This works better than either spraying or changing the water, and merely involves carrying the whole arrangement to a cool spot and placing it on a large wet cloth.

Provided the base of the stems is well covered with water, all silver material does well in shallow containers, but if an accident should occur and a particular piece slips out of water, it can usually be brought back to life in a cup of hot water.

The Plants

CHAPTER 9

THIS is the age of the planner, and many gardeners spend a lot of time designing their borders on paper but lose heart when they see the results. This is probably due to a lack of information about the particular habits and capabilities of the plants. For example, it is quite possible to find out how tall a plant will become, but one usually has to guess how much ground it will cover, with the result that great big gaps develop in one part of the border, while the other end is probably overcrowded.

Then there is the question of peak period, for though all the reference books tell one when to expect a plant to flower, nothing is ever said about when to expect a foliage plant to be at its best. Novices might indeed be forgiven for assuming that when a plant is grown purely for the sake of its foliage, it should remain decorative throughout summer and autumn, but those of us who have watched know only too well that the leaves of silvers, at any rate, have a limited life, and that there are many plants that must be cut back and given a fresh start during the summer months.

The notes which follow are an attempt to cover this sort of query, and the result of watching the behaviour of the plants described, in gardens all over the country. The planting distances are based on the spread that can be expected in one year in gardens near the East coast, and it is possible that those who live in favoured spots in the South may find that they are too close.

So much depends on drainage that it has never been possible to state categorically that any of the silvers were reliably hardy, for even herbaceous Artemisias are quite capable of collapsing when flooded. Trials have shown, however, that the degree of tolerance varies tremendously and that there are greys that can deal with more moisture than others. Some twelve years ago I started to code the plants so that those who had found that they could do a particular subject well could look up its code number, and learn from this which other silvers would be worth trying. This was a great success, and though many of the code numbers have been altered in the light of experience, the system itself has not needed to be changed and it seems to have proved its worth.

Nothing in horticulture is straightforward, and though the code numbers are based on reports of tests carried out in all parts of the country, they do not allow either for areas such as Cumberland, where the rainfall is particularly heavy, or for urban areas where pollution is a serious problem.

1. For plants capable of standing frost pockets and a certain amount of damp.
2. For those that will grow in any ordinary garden soil that does not puddle during periods of thaw.
3. For varieties which will grow on any well drained soil, including well worked clay at the top of a slope.
4. This denotes the old 'half-hardies' which need hot dry beds or tubs. Plants coded 4 survived the winter of 1962–3.
5. For those 'half-hardies' which have survived all the winters except 1962–3 on my well-drained field at Colchester.
6. Definitely for tender plants which, though capable of surviving slight frosts, have not been known to overwinter here.

N.B. Where no advice is given as to the best time for main pruning, no pruning is necessary.

ACAENA *adscendens*

Origin: South America; New Zealand.
Habit: Procumbent. Spreads up to 1 square yard.
Hardiness: 2.
Use: For ground-cover.
Planting time: April–May.
Main pruning: April.
Propagation: Layering in summer.

None of the New Zealand burrs are really grey, but the foliage of *Acaena adscendens* is glaucous and does not look out of place when planted in amongst silvers. Although requiring reasonable drainage, this species is not entirely dependent on direct light and can be used to cover any bare patch of ground, or even the ugly roots of a tree.

The habit is procumbent and extremely vigorous. Young plants are quite capable of throwing out five or six 8″ branches within six weeks of planting. These creep along and usually root into the ground. *A. adscendens* is probably at its most effective when placed on top of a low wall or bank so that the branches can flow down over the edge. The little purple bobbles, which call themselves flowers, are insignificant, but colour is provided by the leaf-bearing stems which turn cherry red as the wood matures.

The plants tend to become clumsy and over-cluttered with age, but can be improved by drastic thinning. This is best done in April but is inclined to produce a surfeit of young shoots, some of which have to be rubbed out as they appear.

From the flower decorator's point of view this is not a particularly outstanding species, for the branches will not take water until the wood is completely mature, and even then they need the hot water treatment. Nevertheless a cluster of purple burrs can sometimes be so placed as to add interest to an otherwise dull bunch of mauve flowers and, from August onwards, it is always possible to find a few branches capable of trailing down over the base of a pedestal.

Propagation presents no problems, for every piece that attaches itself to the ground is a potential young plant and can be moved to another site at any time from April to September. For safety's sake, however, it is advisable to separate the rooted shoot from the parent at least a fortnight before trying to lift it. Young plants should always be stopped when about 6″ tall. If the tip is nipped out at this stage the breaks will come from the bottom, but if it is left to grow, it will merely flop over and produce a whole lot of shoots right up the stem. This does not lead to a manageable specimen!

ACHILLEA *argentea*

Origin: Eastern Alps.
Habit: Cushion. Ht. 6″, allow 12″ width.
Hardiness: 2.
Use: Front edge of borders. Rock gardens.
Planting time: April–June.
Propagation: Division in April. Cuttings in July or April.

Of all the many rock garden Achilleas this is in my opinion the most worthwhile, for the perfect little silver cushion it makes is always bright and cheerful from April through to November. Although of alpine origin, it is a tolerant plant and can be grown in most parts on any reasonably drained land. Young plants take a few months to settle in and seldom cover more than nine inches in their first season. Overcrowding spoils the cushion effect, which is part of the charm of this Achillea, but luckily established plants can be moved in spring.

The pretty little white flowers appear late in May and last for about a fortnight. Their stems are slender and about 6″ long, and as they are good keepers, are often used in small arrangements.

Achillea argentea strikes easily. Cuttings will root in the open if they are taken in summer and covered with a jar, but spring cuttings need bottom heat. The plants can also be increased by division in April.

ACHILLEA 'Moonshine'

Origin: Of garden origin.
Habit: Perennial. Ht. 24″, allow 16″ width.
Hardiness: 1.
Use: Borders and for cutting.
Planting time: October–November. March–April.
Main pruning: March.
Propagation: Division.

Usually listed as *Achillea* 'Moonshine', this variety is more often seen than *Achillea taygetea*, but whether it is actually a better plant is a matter of opinion. Certainly the leaves themselves are longer and the clusters of flowers larger, but it is the hard, somewhat garish yellow of these flowers which may not appeal to everyone, for it is a very difficult colour to place. Nevertheless the long leaves of 'Moonshine' make a superb tussock and many town gardeners have discovered that it can be kept as a silvery mound if the flowering growth is cut out as soon as it starts to run.

ACHILLEA P.D. 166

Origin: Turkey.
Habit: Perennial. Ht. 9″, allow 10″ width.
Hardiness: 2.
Use: Front of border. Rock garden.
Planting time: April–May.
Main pruning: April.
Propagation: Cuttings in July or April.

This Turkish species is just as tough as *A. argentea*, and just as silvery, but though it has been growing here for the past eight years, it has not yet condescended to flower. The crinkly little leaves, seldom more than half an inch long, grow on 8″ stems. Towards the end of July the foliage starts to lose its lustre but a new crop of shoots appears very quickly if the old stems are cut away. Those flower decorators who do small arrangements and miniatures may find this a useful plant, for the tiny leaves take water very quickly and are quite prettily shaped. The habit is upright rather than cushion-forming and very tidy.

Cuttings can be rooted under bell-glasses or jars in summer, but need bottom heat in spring. Division is not a very profitable method of increasing this particular Achillea, for it is seldom possible to make more than four pieces out of each clump.

ACHILLEA *taygetea*

Origin: Levant.
Habit: Perennial. Ht. 24″, allow 16″ width.

Hardiness: 1.
Use: Borders and for cutting.
Planting time: October–November, March–April.
Main pruning: March.
Propagation: Division.

A thoroughly reliable perennial which only requires a sunny, well-drained position and can be grown on any type of soil. The long, fern-shaped leaves are soft grey and form tidy tussocks about 8″ tall. These tussocks are quite decorative in themselves but are seldom seen, for *Achillea taygetea* is nearly always covered with flowering stems. These vary in length from 18″ to 2′ and carry flat clusters of pale yellow flowers. The summer crop starts to open in June and continues through to the middle of August. If the plants are regularly dead-headed, this is followed by another spectacular show in autumn which continues through to winter.

This Achillea is of some value to the flower decorator, both for the sake of its leaves which are very graceful, and for the sake of its flowers. The foliage needs no special hardening provided it is reasonably mature. The flowers last well and do not lose much of their colour when dried in the dark.

Achillea taygetea is easy to propagate for it is always possible to detach a shoot with a root from the outside of the clump without even bothering to dig up the parent. If this is done in September the young plant will work its way into the soil before the arrival of winter and should grow on without trouble. In October, however, it is safer to pot up all the off-sets and leave them to grow on quietly in a cold greenhouse or covered frame, for there is some evidence to suggest that the base of a shoot will rot if it gets too wet before the root has taken hold.

ANAPHALIS *nubigena*

Origin: Himalayas.
Habit: Perennial. Ht. 12″, allow 12″ width.
Hardiness: 1.
Use: Borders and for drying.
Planting time: Autumn or Spring.
Propagation: Division in Autumn or Spring.

This perennial is closely allied to *A. triplinervis* and just as hardy, but smaller in all ways. It may, therefore, be a better choice for the small garden as it can be planted at twelve inches and seldom exceeds 14″ in height. For cutting, however, it is somewhat disappointing as very few of the stems exceed 8″.

ANAPHALIS *triplinervis*

Origin: Himalayas.
Habit: Perennial. Ht. 16″, allow 14″ width.
Hardiness: 1.
Use: Borders and for drying.
Planting time: Autumn or Spring.
Propagation: Division in Autumn or Spring.

Commonly known as the 'Pearly Immortelle', this ultra-hardy perennial makes a tidy clump of silver in spring and early summer but changes character in August, when it covers its foliage with a wealth of flowering stems.

The pearly-white everlasting flowers are loosely clustered into flat heads and have ten-inch stems. They open in early September but remain decorative throughout autumn. Although these flowers are at their most attractive while they are still in bud, it is fatal to try cutting them at this stage, for their stems are still immature and will not take water. Once the centres of the flowers can be seen, however, they will last for a year. Those required for drying should always be given a drink before being hung upside down in loose bunches. If this is done, the flowers retain their form perfectly.

Although *A. triplinervis* will strike easily, a single root can be divided into so many pieces that it is seldom necessary to worry about cuttings.

ANTENNARIA *aprica*

Origin: S. Europe. Asia.
Habit: Carpeting perennial. Allow 9″ width.
Hardiness: 3.
Use: As a silver carpet.
Planting time: April–May.
Propagation: Division.

The foliage of this species forms a tight carpet of silver rosettes which gradually spread over the ground. The pinky white flowers are virtually everlasting, but too small and flimsy for most designs. *Antennaria aprica* can look very attractive in a trough, especially when it is allowed to creep down over the edge.

When extra plants are required it is merely a question of feeling the carpet to find out which pieces have rooted into the ground, and then cutting them out. This is best done in April so that the young plants have the advantage of warm soil. Slugs are rather fond of all carpeting Antennarias but can generally be spotted as they pull down the leaf to which they have attached themselves.

ANTENNARIA *dioica minima*

Origin: Europe, Asia and N. America.
Habit: Carpeting perennial. Allow 9″–12″ width.
Hardiness: 3.
Use: As a silver carpet.
Planting time: April–May.
Propagation: Division.

The perfect silver carpet either for the rock garden or for the front edge of a border, although perhaps it is really at its best when allowed to wander over a brick path. On well drained soil it makes a tight mat of little rosettes, seldom more than an inch above the ground. This mat retains its silver appearance throughout summer and early autumn though it turns green in winter. The fairy-like pink flowers, borne on slender 6″ stems, are nearly everlasting and in perfect scale. It is difficult to suggest how much room to leave each plant to cover for much depends on how quickly they settle in, but this is a species which can be transplanted very easily so it is probably better not to allow more than 9″ to begin with.

Although it is always possible to make a great number of young plants by dividing a well established clump, it is usually more practical to take a few rosettes, complete with roots, from the outside of the parent plant and pot them up.

ANTHEMIS *rudolphiana*

Origin:	Garden, possibly a selected form of biebersteinii.
Habit:	Cushion-forming perennial. Ht. 8″, allow 12″ width.
Hardiness:	1.
Use:	Front edge of borders. Rockery. Leaves for decoration.
Planting time:	Autumn or Spring.
Main pruning:	None necessary. Remove dead leaves in March.
Propagation:	Division in Autumn.

A member of the Camomile family, this hardy, cushion-forming perennial can stand more moisture than most silvers. The finely cut foliage is bright in early summer when the leaves are young but tends to become somewhat drab as the year wears on. To a certain extent this can be prevented if some of the shoots carrying the flowering stems are cut right back to within two inches of the ground when the flowers have faded. This induces breaks, which should have grown good leaves in time to hide some of the worn out foliage in August. Unfortunately, however miserable they may appear, the old leaves do not drop off but can be pulled off easily.

Although the bright yellow daisy-like flowers are quite gay when seen on the plants in late May, they are disappointing when cut. The foliage, however, is of considerable value to the flower decorator, for the finely cut leaves are about 5″ long and always have good stems. When growing, they flow outwards from the heart of the plant towards the ground, and when cut have a distinct curve. These leaves keep well and no special hardening drill is called for.

Anthemis rudolphiana will not root from a cutting, but as it is the easiest plant to split, and as a twelve month old plant can often be broken down into thirty pieces, this is of little importance. Division is more successful when undertaken in autumn.

Many northern gardeners grow *Anthemis biebersteinii* in preference to *A. rudolphiana* but I have never been able to see why, for it is certainly not so grey and could not be much hardier.

ARTEMISIA *absinthium* 'Lambrook Silver'

Origin: Garden (developed from the native Wormwood).
Habit: Shrub. Ht. 2' 6" when in flower. Allow 18" width.
Hardiness: 1.
Use: Middle of the border and for cutting.
Planting time: Autumn and Spring.
Main pruning: April.
Propagation: Cuttings in July.

It is many years since the late Mrs. Margery Fish first spotted that one plant, growing in amongst a clump of Artemisia, had particularly bright silvery foliage. Since then 'Lambrook Silver' has become one of the best loved border plants as well as a happy reminder of a great gardener.

It is a good shrub in every sense of the word, for it is extremely hardy and quite capable of dealing with all kinds of soil, including clay. In early May the plant is covered with pale green shoots which soon become grey. By June these shoots turn into clusters of silver carrot-shaped leaves, but in less than a month they change again into 18" wands, heavily festooned with tiny yellow bobbles. When these are cut down after flowering, the leaves, which retain their lustre throughout, continue growing until they are as big as a man's hand. These large leaves remain in good condition for several months and seem to cascade down the sides of the plant.

When in flower, 'Lambrook Silver' may measure $2\frac{1}{2}'$ from the ground but, when shorn of its stems, the bush is unlikely to be more than 16" tall. It needs to spread over at least 18". Summer storms are inclined to batter down the flowering stems but staking does not do much to prevent this.

Pruning is merely a question of cutting away most of the previous year's growth. This can be done in early April for, even if the breaks do meet with a frost, they are unlikely to come to much harm.

The carrot-shaped leaves cannot be hardened satisfactorily until August, but from then onwards a lot of useful leaves can be cut from each plant and these need no special treatment if they are put into water quickly. They are easy to place as they always grow on good stalks. In July the flowering stems will keep well if their ends are put into hot water as soon as they are cut, but they are inclined to be clumsy and it is the weaker stems which grow on the sides of the plant which are the most decorative. Once hardened, these stems can be dried and do best if they are hung upside down in very small bunches.

Artemisia 'Lambrook Silver' is such an essential for anyone interested in silvers that it is sad to have to state that it is difficult to propagate. The only method is by cuttings and these can be temperamental. There is a moment in July when 4″ shoots, complete with four pairs of leaves, can be found at the base of mature flowering stems. Sometimes these will strike without a murmur, but in certain seasons the losses are very heavy. Cuttings must always be taken with a woody heel and inserted into sand just as quickly as possible for they flag the moment they are taken off the parent. Difficulty in propagation accounts for the scarcity of this grand plant in the trade, for even with bottom heat it is still somewhat unreliable.

In old days bunches of Wormwood were hung up to repel flies, and it does seem that there is something about the musty smell which flies dislike, for when I kept a spray in my kitchen I never saw a fly. The only trouble was that I disliked the smell as much as the flies!

ARTEMISIA *arborescens*

Origin:	Mediterranean. Southern Europe.
Habit:	Upright shrub. Ht. 3′, allow 2′ 6″ width.
Hardiness:	4.
Use:	Middle to back of border.
Planting time:	May–June.
Main pruning:	Mid-May onwards.
Propagation:	Cuttings in Summer. Layering in Summer.

This shrub, probably the most beautiful of all the silvers, needs perfect drainage and must only be attempted on light soil. Its charm lies entirely in the beauty of its silky foliage which, in summer, has a silvery sheen seldom seen in other plants. The flowering stems, generally few and far between, have no decorative value whatsoever and should be removed.

Young plants need a lot of stopping in their first summer if they are to become perfect specimens in the future. Assuming that a plant

79

has been stopped before being put out, the best treatment is to nip each shoot back to two nodes as soon as it has made six or seven leaves. In August all the shoots can be left to grow on in peace so that the wood has time to mature before winter. Stopped plants seldom cover more than a square foot in their first year, but thereafter they may, with luck, spread over four square feet. Once planted, the strong roots are not easy to move and this is a particularly difficult subject to transplant.

Artemisia arborescens suffers badly if its young shoots are caught by a frost, and in most parts of the country pruning is best delayed until the second half of May. How much to cut away depends entirely on the position occupied by the shrub, for though this species will break if it is pruned right down to a stump, this sort of treatment does not produce a very graceful specimen, and it is often better just to shorten the previous year's growth back to two eyes.

By late summer the foliage loses its brilliance, but the weather-worn leaves can be hidden behind a crop of fresh young sprigs if the tops of some of the stems are nipped back in July. This does not spoil the appearance of the shrub for it is only necessary to cut away the first three or four leaves. The clusters of shoots break out very quickly and, as they do not have to fight their way through to the light, usually become silvery straight away.

Artemisia arborescens is of little or no value for cutting. It is true that mature foliage will harden in August, but the lovely silky pieces which would look so gorgeous in July arrangements will not respond to any known hardening technique and always flag as soon as they are cut.

This Artemisia is generally propagated from cuttings, but can also be increased by layers, which should be pegged down early in July. Cuttings are temperamental but will usually root in sand if they are taken with a heel in summer. Shoots about 5″ in length will strike if

PLATE I
1 Artemisia "Lambrook Silver"
2 Artemisia purshiana
3 Artemisia stelleriana
4 Artemisia nutans
5 Artemisia arborescens

4

5

3

they are not allowed to flag. Once the foliage has gone limp it seldom recovers and this usually results in the failure of the cutting. Cuttings taken very early in the morning and planted straight away always have the best chance.

ARTEMISIA *discolor*

Origin: Western North America.
Habit: Sub-shrub with running root. Ht. 18″, allow 12″ width.
Hardiness: 2.
Use: For ground-cover.
Planting time: Spring.
Main pruning: April.
Propagation: From runners.

This feathery sub-shrub is perfectly hardy and can be grown on most kinds of soil, but it is somewhat invasive. Provided it is not placed near anything valuable, it has its value, however, for the foliage is almost white, and certainly a lot paler than that of most Artemisias. It seems to have no other bad habits and can be used in conjunction with the more solid *Artemisia purshiana* to clothe a rough area. The flowering spikes are very stiff and formal, and it is the younger growth which attracts attention. A constant succession of this is ensured if the smaller spikes are removed from time to time and this is really all that is necessary to keep the foliage of this species going.

From the flower decorator's point of view *Artemisia discolor* is not worth growing, for though the spikes will harden, they are not very decorative, and there is no way of persuading a fluffy sprig, however attractive, to take water. Enthusiastic plantsmen though, might well try potting a plant, for it can be grown into a very lovely cloud of silver.

It is always easy to find runners with shoots attached and each of these can be transplanted, so there is no real need to strike cuttings though shoots taken from the base in July root very quickly.

ARTEMISIA *glacialis*

Origin:	Mountains of Central Europe.
Habit:	Carpeting shrublet. Ht. 3″, allow 12″ width.
Hardiness:	3–4.
Use:	Rockery.
Planting time:	May.
Propagation:	Layering in Summer.

A little treasure which spreads out into a ground-hugging mat. It needs very sharp drainage and a completely open position and cannot therefore be grown either in wet or in urban areas. The foliage is bright and feathery and the small silver sprigs are often the first signs of spring, for *Artemisia glacialis* seems to make a habit of pushing its way through the snow in February. The growth is probably too slow for this species to be used for edging borders, but it is a superb rock garden plant, and seems to enjoy creeping over rocks.

The flowers, which come on 6″ stems, are not impressive and tend to spoil the smooth appearance of the carpet, but they do not appear to damage the foliage. The roots of this Artemisia are not very strong, and it is easy to hurt them when weeding, especially when couch, bellbind or grasses have to be dragged out. Young plants need regular hand-weeding and it is advisable to inspect the established mats fairly regularly so that all weeds can be removed before the plants have developed a fibrous root system.

The only other thing which can spoil the appearance of this gem is to strip its woody stems of shoots for cuttings, as once these have been removed there is little chance that they will be replaced. However, it is not really necessary to worry about striking cuttings as most of the ground-hugging leads root themselves into the ground in any case and can be lifted without trouble. When more plants are required, all the outer leads can be layered with very little difficulty for it is only a question of covering the woody part of the stems with an inch or two of soil, patting it down firmly and waiting for a month! Speedier rooting can be ensured if the top two inches of soil is loosened and mixed with a little sand.

ARTEMISIA *lanata pedemontana*

Origin: Mountains of Central and Southern Europe.
Habit: Spreading shrublet. Ht. 6″, allow 12″ width.
Hardiness: 2.
Use: Rockery and edging.
Planting time: May.
Propagation: Layering.

Sound stocks of this enchanting shrublet are perfectly hardy and only need reasonable drainage, but there are some weak strains in circulation which will not even stand a winter in a well drained rock garden! In appearance this is really a larger version of *Artemisia glacialis* and hugs the ground in much the same manner but it has thicker foliage and makes a deeper carpet. Every year it is a joy in winter and early spring, for the young shoots often start to appear in January. By habit it is very tidy and makes a cheerful, feathery edging for a border. As a plant for a newly constructed rock garden it is quite invaluable and does not take long to drape itself over bare rocks. Furthermore, the glistening silver foliage makes a perfect background for spring bulbs.

The flowers are as poor as those of most of the family and are not really worth keeping, but as they do not seem to affect the foliage in any way need not be cut off.

Weeds are as bad for *Artemisia lanata pedemontana* as they are for *A. glacialis*. Their roots are very easily torn and it is essential to hand-weed round the plants when they are young. Blades of grass etc. must always be removed as soon as they are seen, for once grass or weed roots of any kind have spread out and got a hold on the soil they cannot be pulled out without disturbance.

This Artemisia can be used to cover the ugly woody base of a plant, such as a Pink, which has just been layered for it is not greedy and can therefore be planted right up against the bare wood of another plant. As the silver shoots spread out, so they will cover the ugly stems with a tidy carpet without damaging the layers.

As for propagating, *Artemisia lanata pedemontana* is self-layering, and by running a finger gently round the outside of a clump, it is usually possible to find several shoots which have dug themselves into the ground. If no roots can be found they can always be encouraged if a handful of soil is thrown on to some of the woody stems of the ground hugging leads. The soil must, of course, be made reasonably firm, but should not be over consolidated.

Cuttings will root in sand in July without heat, but taking too many off one parent will do it no good for most of the best short-jointed shoots come from the centre and, once they have been taken, the plant is left with a nasty bald patch which it can never cover.

ARTEMISIA *ludoviciana*

Origin: North America.
Habit: Invasive perennial. Ht. 24″, allow 9″ width.
Hardiness: 1.
Use: For clothing rough patches. For cutting.
Planting time: Autumn or Spring.
Main pruning: Spring.
Propagation: Division or runners.

This may be a very beautiful plant in summer when its foliage is bright silver, but its roots are as invasive as those of couch grass and, once established, they are quite as difficult to eradicate. So it is not a good subject for a border filled with treasures.

Nevertheless there are plots in most gardens which cannot be fully tended, and *Artemisia ludoviciana* can do a useful job as ground cover in these positions. It is true that the patch will have to be weeded until the young plants have developed, but once they have become established there are not many weeds capable of pushing their way through the dense canopy of grey foliage. In order to get a good cover it is best to plant at 9″. The plumes of flowers, carried on 24″ stems, are at their best in July. These flowers are of no particular value but, as the stems are heavily felted, the overall impression of a flowering clump is that of pale silvery grey. Unfortunately, a day of thunderstorms can make a sad difference, and when the plants have been bashed to the ground it is best to scythe them down and wait for another crop of fresh growth. Incidentally, this can be done with the kind of mechanical cutter used for rough grass.

Flowering stems of *Artemisia ludoviciana* can be hardened once the tiny petals of the flowers have opened. At this stage they are easy to handle and need no special treatment, but if the flowers are still in bud the soft wood at the base of the stem must be singed. Non-flowering growth will not often harden and for the flower decorator this is not as useful a subject as *A. purshiana*. Propagation is by division either in autumn or spring but, when only a few plants are needed, it is easier to lift some wandering shoots out of the ground with a trowel, for they are bound to have plenty of root.

ARTEMISIA *nutans*

Origin:	Sicily and the Canary Islands.
Habit:	Shrub. Ht. 18″, allow 9″ width.
Hardiness:	1.
Use:	Centre of border.
Planting time:	Autumn or Spring.
Main pruning:	April.
Propagation:	Cuttings in June/July or April.

There is some similarity between the lacy foliage of this shrub and that of *Artemisia discolor* but the great difference is that the root of this species is not invasive so it can be planted in the border near to valuable plants.

There are exceptions to most rules and this certainly applies to *Artemisia nutans* for, unlike most silvers, it does better on heavy soil than it does on light.

The foliage is light and flimsy and the plants throw up a multitude of thin silvery stems not more than eighteen inches tall, none of which carry many leaves. Eventually these stems run up to graceful flowering spikes, but the general effect continues to be luminous until the flowers have actually faded and started to seed. This usually happens in August and, though a second crop of foliage can be encouraged to grow if the old stems are cut away, the plants never try to flower again so that the second crop of shoots seldom grows to more than 10″.

A single specimen of *Artemisia nutans* is a skinny-looking object and, to get the best out of this species, several plants need to be seen together. By planting at 9″, the stems can intermingle and this helps them to withstand the wind.

Most Artemisias have aromatic leaves but the scent of this species is outstanding for, without being in the least pungent, it is quite capable of clearing a stuffy head. Many years ago, when my daughter was recovering from a riding accident, I found all the leaves disappearing from *A. nutans* and thought that there must be a caterpillar at work. It was only later that I discovered a large collection of leaves in her pocket and realised that she was running to the plant whenever she had a headache.

The lacy shoots will not harden until they have elongated into flowering stems. This really means that *Artemisia nutans* is not a very useful plant for cutting as these flower spikes are so light and fairy-like that their value is distinctly limited.

Cuttings can be found in June and early July at the base of each stem. Short jointed shoots about 4″ in length root best. In spring it is possible to strike the first few breaks which appear in April, but these will need bottom heat.

ARTEMISIA *purshiana*

Origin:	Western North America.
Habit:	Invasive herbaceous perennial. Ht. 12″. Plant at 9″.
Hardiness:	1.
Use:	For ground cover and for cutting.
Planting time:	Autumn or Spring.
Main pruning:	Early Spring.
Propagation:	Division or runners.

There are several forms of this Artemisia, some a great deal better than others. The shoots of a good type should be grey from the moment they appear and by May the foliage and stems should have become near-white. There are, however, some strains about which start green and remain dull and dingy throughout the entire summer.

The shoots start to run in July and, as the stems are heavily felted, the plants remain attractive throughout their flowering season. As with so many other subjects, the leaves lose their lustre as soon as the flowers wither and the plants themselves eventually become very untidy if they are not cut down. Curiously enough, this species seems to need some moisture in the soil if it is to produce a good second crop of foliage and, in dry years, it is advisable to give the plants a good flooding when they are trimmed down. The second crop never tries to run to flower and can be a lovely sight in autumn.

Were it not for the invasive habits of its roots *Artemisia purshiana* would be a perfect choice for any border, and those who own cold difficult gardens would be well advised to consider allowing it a place amongst other plants, for with care it is possible to control it. The habit of the plant is to stretch its roots out in all directions, but these do not go far before revealing themselves by throwing up a cluster of shoots. If the ground between the plant and the cluster is loosened with a fork, it is perfectly easy to remove the whole of the wandering root.

As a ground cover there are few plants more certain to swamp weeds and, if a shorter cover is required, it can be used instead of *A. ludoviciana* for rough patches.

The flowering stems are nearly white, but the actual flowers small and insignificant. As outline material for flower decorations the pointed panicles of flowers are invaluable, for they are neither too light nor too heavy and harden readily. It is, however, not necessary to wait for a leafy stalk to produce flowers before cutting it, for once the bark at the base has become woody, the stem will take water. Softer wood is somewhat unreliable but in July it is often possible to find a fair number of very prettily foliated shoots, about 12″ long and these will generally keep if they are singed.

As with *A. ludoviciana* this species can be divided but is usually propagated by runners, which will strike at any time of year if their roots are not allowed to dry out.

ARTEMISIA *schmidtiana*

Origin:	Japan.
Habit:	Herbaceous cushion. Ht. 9″, allow 18″ width.
Hardiness:	2.
Use:	Front of border. Rockery.
Planting time:	May.
Main pruning:	April.
Propagation:	Division. Summer cuttings.

When seen from a distance in early summer *Artemisia schmidtiana* looks just like a moss-covered molehill, but in actual fact the cushion is very flimsy, being made up of a quantity of lacy sprigs, all springing from the heart of the plant.

It is a very easy subject to grow, but just as easy to dig up in error. Most herbaceous perennials leave something above the ground when they are cut down, but the stems of *Artemisia schmidtiana* are so threadlike that they are hard to spot against damp ground, and plants that have been cut back in autumn usually come to a sticky end.

Nobody can foretell when the first breaks will appear in spring. Sometimes a strong cluster will push its way through the ground in February, but there is nothing to worry about if the plants do not show any signs of life until early in May.

The shoots are a pale green to begin with and never turn a true grey, but remain green overlaid with silver. After flowering in July the foliage becomes dowdy and the stems flop over to reveal a bunch of fresh pale green sprigs. If the old growth is cut away so that these young shoots can develop, the general appearance of the plants can be just as good in August and September as it was in June.

There is no trick which will prevent a herbaceous subject going to earth for the winter, but *Artemisia schmidtiana* does at least put on a lovely display at the end of the season when it turns russet red and stays like this for at least three weeks.

Propagation by division is not a quick way of increasing this Artemisia, for the crowns are never very large. The breaks which come from the centre of the plant make good cuttings, however, and should be taken when about 3″ long. In summer, these can be rooted under jars, but in spring they need bottom heat.

ARTEMISIA *splendens*

Origin:	Armenia. Caucasus. Persia.
Habit:	Woody stemmed perennial. Ht. 18″, allow 18″ width.
Hardiness:	2.
Use:	For borders.
Planting time:	April–May.
Main pruning:	April.
Propagation:	Cuttings and runners.

Though this Artemisia is sufficiently graceful for single specimens to have their charm, this is really a subject to plant in thin drifts which

88

can be seen from a distance, for it is only then that one can really appreciate the misty effect of the pale silver foliage.

Individual leaves of *Artemisia splendens* are so curly and so finely cut that they might well be made out of the strands of an old-fashioned aluminium pot scourer. In spring the green breaks come from a woody base and start by growing outwards. Very shortly the young leaves turn grey and at the same time the shoots begin to straighten themselves up towards the sky. As each mature plant carries about sixteen well-feathered stems, the effect is impressive, nor is it spoilt when the tips of the stems start to elongate into spikes. The flowers, of course, are totally insignificant, but the silhouette of a plant in flower is interesting and I do not think that the spikes should be cut down until the leaves have started to lose their lustre in August. It is a plant which breaks easily and there is always a plentiful supply of young growth waiting in the wings.

Propagation is by cuttings, usually found at the base of each flowering stem in July. These are seldom more than 3″ long and must be rooted under a jar. The breaks which come through in spring can also be used, but are usually very soft, and are not very easy to strike, even with heat. Although not invasive, just occasionally a root will throw out a runner and it is always well worth searching for the young sprig which might have a root.

ARTEMISIA *stelleriana*

Origin:	North East Asia. Eastern North America.
Habit:	Spreading perennial. Ht. 12″, allow 14″ width.
Hardiness:	1.
Use:	Border. Ground cover.
Planting time:	Spring and Autumn.
Propagation:	Layering. Cuttings.

Amongst Artemisias *stelleriana* is undoubtedly the odd man out, for its solid near-white leaves are similar in form to those of a chrysanthemum and even have much the same smell. Furthermore, the plant itself can stand more wet and shade than any other of the Artemisias. Though not invasive, it has naturalised itself at Marazion in Cornwall.

Young plants could easily be taken for chrysanthemum cuttings which had been allowed to develop mildew, but their stems are weak, and if left unstopped always flops over before the plant is 6″ tall. As soon as this happens a single break starts to grow straight up from the base, but it, in turn, falls over as soon as it reaches 6″. This is the natural habit, but it does not lead to tidiness for, once the stems are lying on the ground, they all produce their own side-breaks and these very soon become tangled. It is, I think, wiser to stop the first lead as soon as it is possible to leave four nodes, but before it falls over. Three good breaks should appear and if the plant is to be used as ground cover, these can be allowed to drape themselves out over the ground. As they grow, the tips of the stems and breaks turn up towards the light, so that the rosettes of white leaves show to their full advantage.

In late July some of the rosettes lengthen out into flowering spikes. The creamy flowers are slightly larger than those of most Artemisias and grow up close to the stem, which is very downy and somewhat solid, but seldom exceeds 10″ in length.

Throughout the season fresh shoots keep on growing out of the centre so that though each piece does eventually tumble over towards the ground, the plant is never left bare. Tidying is therefore merely a matter of removing any worn-out leads, as and when necessary.

Artemisia stelleriana can be grown as a specimen bush if it is staked early in life and treated as a summer flowering chrysanthemum. The first stopping of a young plant should be done in April and should leave at least four nodes. Thereafter each shoot must be stopped as soon as it is possible to leave three nodes. Some fairly loose ties of raffia will be needed from time to time, but plants which have been treated in this manner are rewarding, for by mid-July they resemble, at a distance, large specimens of *Senecio cineraria* but are, of course, a great deal easier to manage on heavy soil. In the second and subsequent years it is essential to rub out all but three shoots before starting to train the plants for summer.

Artemisia stelleriana is not a particularly useful plant for the decorator although, from time to time, it is possible to find some attractive bits which will harden. The flowering stems take water very easily, but the rosettes of leaves, which would make such perfect centres for all-foliage designs, will not take water if the cut is made into soft wood. Hence, though it might be perfectly safe to use a leafy piece with a stem 10″ long, if the same piece were shortened to 6″, it would probably wilt.

Propagation is easy, for 5″ cuttings taken from the centre will root at most times of year, and any procumbent lead which has not run to flower, will strike, even if it is layered with a minimum of expertise.

ARTEMISIA *tridentata*

Origin:	Western North America.
Habit:	Shrub. Ht. 4′, allow 2′ width.
Hardiness:	3.
Use:	For the back of border.
Planting time:	May.
Main pruning:	May.
Propagation:	Cuttings.

This, the American Sage bush, is slow growing and not a particularly exciting shrub, but the scent of its leaves is delicious and it is well worth planting a bush just for the sake of brushing up against its branches.

The foliage is quite a good grey, each leaf being about half an inch long. The branches are closely packed with these little leaves and very stiff in appearance, and I have yet to find out how to prune this plant in order to make it appear graceful. Perhaps the answer is to thin it from the centre so that its main branches can stand out. For the sake of appearance the wispy flowering stems should certainly come off, for they merely look untidy and never seem to belong to the shrub.

These wispy pieces, however, are highly aromatic and quite a small bunch will scent a room. Some say that flies will not come near *Artemisia tridentata*, but I have found no evidence of this. Propagation is difficult, but pieces of semi-mature wood, taken with a heel in August, will often strike. The young plants, however, are not very hardy and need to spend their first winter in a frame.

ATRIPLEX *canescens*

Origin: Western North America.
Habit: Shrub. Ht. 4′, allow 30″ width.
Hardiness: 3.
Use: Back of border.
Planting time: April–May.
Main pruning: April–May.
Propagation: Layers or cuttings.

Though this is not such a good silver as *Atriplex halimus* and is certainly not nearly as useful for cutting, it has the great advantage that it does not seem to attract the birds in the same way, and can therefore be grown inland.

Its main failing is that the leaves are thin and wispy, and that the branches themselves are not particularly heavily foliated, so that the shrub does not give a clear-cut impression of grey. Nevertheless, it is one of the few silvers which will grow to any sort of height, and is therefore often used at the back of borders.

No pruning will thicken out the branches and it is probably best left to its own devices once it has been cut back in April. It can be propagated by 3″ cuttings taken with a heel in July, or it can be layered. The latter is probably the easiest, for the layers can be left attached to the plant for the winter, while rooted cuttings would probably be too soft to be left in the open garden.

ATRIPLEX *halimus*

Origin: Southern Europe. Naturalised in Jersey and on
                 South Coast.
Habit: Shrub. Ht. 5′, allow 3′ width.
Hardiness: 2. Seaside gardens only.
Use: Back of border.
Planting time: April–May.
Main pruning: April.
Propagation: Cuttings.

Always a good silvery shrub when planted near to the sea, this can be a sad disappointment inland as, for some reason, it always gets stripped of its foliage by birds. For some time I wondered whether it might be the host for some tasty caterpillar, but this was disproved by a flock of birds who found a few trial plants growing under glass and attacked them viciously, leaving everything else intact. All the plants in the house had been sprayed and had been carefully inspected for caterpillars before the attack took place!

Although *Atriplex halimus* seldom flowers, it does need some cutting back in summer if it is to remain decorative for it has a habit of shedding some of the leaves from the tip of each branch, as those who have seen it growing wild in Jersey may have noticed. 'Tipping' can be done at any time in summer.

For flower arrangers who crave for long shapely branches of grey foliage, there is nothing to compare with this Atriplex, and branches will keep for weeks once they have been given the hot water treatment.

Propagation is by 3″ cuttings taken with a heel in July. These root quickly and can usually be left to overwinter in the open garden.

BALLOTA *pseudodictamnus*

Origin:	Crete.
Habit:	Woody perennial. Ht. 2′, allow 2′ width.
Hardiness:	3.
Use:	Border and as ground cover for sunny shrubberies.
Planting time:	April–May.
Main pruning:	May.
Propagation:	Cuttings.

As with people, so with plants. There are some who do not impress at first sight, but who gradually worm their way into one's affections and make themselves indispensable. Ballota is such a plant. Essentially demure, it is always a pleasant sight and one that always does its job to the best of its ability.

In spring the woody base of established plants is smothered with countless rosettes of pale apple green leaves. These gradually grow into 18″ stems. The lower leaves on each stem remain apple green but those near the tip develop more and more wool as the sun becomes hotter and eventually become nearly white. Towards the end of June the whorls start to show up the stems. Starting from the bottom each leaf axil has its own whorl of pale green bracts. The flowers, when they do open in July, are actually mauve, but so small that they are practically invisible. As the whorls at the top of the stems start to swell, the leaves at the bottom of the stems begin to shrivel, and shortly afterwards the entire stem becomes untidy and cries out to be removed.

But *Ballota pseudodictamnus* is always making fresh growth, and though this may seem very green when it is first uncovered, it grows quickly and does not take long to turn white. Sometimes a few of these secondaries may try to flower in autumn, but more often they stay as cheerful rosettes of leaves throughout the winter. It takes a hard winter to denude this species of its leaves but when this has happened it may take a time before the plant is able to make a new start. After the hard winter of 1963 no signs of life could be seen on fifty specimens till the last week in May and then they all started sprouting together.

In shape this perennial is always bush-like and it has the virtue of always clothing itself right down to the ground, so that it is never leggy.

It is when *Ballota pseudodictamnus* is grown for cutting that the 'cut and come again' habit is really appreciated, for every time a stem is cut another rushes up to take its place. These stems make good outline material, sometimes 20″ in length, and harden readily, though it is true that the tips will flag when the wood is not completely mature. As a guide, once the tiny mauve flowers can be seen inside the lower bracts, the wood will take water. If a tip does happen to flag when cut, the only answer is to nip it out, and if this is done immediately above a whorl the scar will not show, though the stem will be somewhat shorter.

Many decorators use dried Ballota as they would Mollucella, and though both stems and whorls are much smaller, it can be very decorative. Bunches to be dried must always be given a long drink before they are hung up. Ideally, they should be kept in the dark and certainly keep their colour better when hung upside down.

Propagation is by cuttings, which root easily enough in July when taken with a heel. Young plants, however, are inclined to collapse in wet winters, and should therefore be kept in a frame till April.

CALOCEPHALUS *brownii*
(*Leucophytum brownii*)

Origin:	Australia.
Habit:	Shrub. Ht. 12–18".
Hardiness:	6.
Use:	Greenhouse and bedding.
Planting time:	May.
Propagation:	Cuttings.

Perhaps the best way of describing this plant would be to compare it to a neat little bundle of twigs dipped in a bath of silver paint, for it is actually the stems and twiglets which are so silvery rather than the minute leaves.

There is some argument about the meaning of the name. Some would say that it was 'beautiful head' and others that it meant 'antlered head'. If the former, it would be difficult to understand for though the $\frac{1}{2}$" flowers are reminiscent of the sort of gilt bobbles that are worn as beads, they are not particularly beautiful. If, on the other hand, Calocephalus does mean 'the antlered head' this makes more sense for the twiglets are shaped like antlers.

Although often used as a bedding plant it is not really suitable for the open garden for it does not grow very fast and is killed by the mildest frost. However, it makes a very pretty little pot plant and will trail when planted in a hanging basket.

Propagation is by 2" cuttings rooted in bottom heat at any time of the year. Without heat it is difficult to persuade these cuttings to strike.

CENTAUREA *gymnocarpa* 'Colchester White'

Origin:	Corsica.
Habit:	Sub-shrub. Ht. 18"–24", allow 18" width.
Hardiness:	5.
Use:	Border. Greenhouse.
Planting time:	May.
Main pruning:	After flowering.
Propagation:	Cuttings.

Many years ago I came across a very old specimen of *Centaurea gymnocarpa* growing up beside a wall in a derelict garden in Essex. Knowing that this species was not considered hardy, I grew on some cuttings and left them outside for the following winter. For several years all was well, but then came the hard winter and the collapse of all the outdoor plants. So a fresh stock had to be raised from a few indoor specimens and it is interesting to note that these have never been quite so hardy and will only survive when planted on top of banks.

This is a tragedy, for *Centaurea gymnocarpa* is different from all other silvers in shape and form and extremely handsome once it has reached maturity.

In young plants, the long, deeply indented white leaves do not have a chance of showing their true beauty, for once they are fully grown, they curl over and trail on the ground. As the plant ages, however, it grows upwards in the manner of a palm, and this allows the leaves to be properly displayed. Luckily the roots of *Centaurea gymnocarpa* can stand a lot of maltreatment. An established plant will always consent to being lifted for the winter, even if it has been planted directly into the border. Centaureas are easier to move, however, when originally planted in 6″ pots which can be eased out of the ground in autumn and stood in a dry greenhouse. No heat is necessary.

The sprays of mauve flowers are very decorative and do not seem to interfere with the flow of sap to the leaves. Their stems come from the heart of the plant, and at dead-heading time it is important to see that every little bit of stalk is removed, for otherwise they will go on trying to produce more and more flowers.

The ordinary *Centaurea gymnocarpa* can be raised from seed sown early in February, but 'Colchester White', which was chosen for its hardiness, must be raised from cuttings. In July a mature plant should be showing a number of side shoots, roughly 4″–6″ in length. These will root well enough with slight bottom heat, but must have their leaves shortened back before they are inserted, otherwise these will trail on to the sand and fall victims to botrytis.

CENTAUREA *ragusina*

Origin:	Crete.
Habit:	Perennial. Allow 7″ width.
Hardiness:	6.
Use:	Summer bedding or in greenhouse.
Planting time:	May.
Propagation:	Seed.

Young specimens of this half-hardy perennial are often seen in bedding displays and are ideal for the purpose for their narrow 8″ leaves grow up from the base and are almost dead white. Most plants improve in appearance as they reach maturity but the habit of this Centaurea is to go on covering its worn-out foliage with young leaves so that eventually it becomes distinctly leggy. Under glass it can, of course, be cut back, but for garden decoration it is certainly better to rely on seedlings.

This Centaurea is not very interested in flowering and seedlings seldom run up in their first summer, whilst older specimens are usually content to throw just one hideous, dandelion-like flower and call it a day when it is chopped off.

The leaves of this Centaurea are not only white but are also perfectly shaped for decorative work and grow on 2″ stems. Unfortunately young plants do not carry a great number of leaves and it is seldom possible to remove many without leaving ugly gaps.

The seed germinates very readily if sown in February. If the seedlings are potted into 3″ pots as soon as the first true leaf shows they should be ready to plant out in May.

PLATE II
1   Ballota pseudodictamnus
2   Gazania 'Silver Beauty'
3   Teucrium fruticans
4   Tanacetum densum amanum

CHRYSANTHEMUM *ptarmacaefolium*

(*Pyrethrum ptarmacaefolium*)

Origin:	Teneriffe.
Habit:	Shrub. Ht. 18″–2′.
Hardiness:	6.
Use:	Greenhouse.
Potting time:	March
Main pruning:	Summer.
Propagation:	Seed or cuttings.

Although classified as hardy in certain lists, this Chrysanthemum has never yet managed to get through a winter in the Colchester area and I would certainly not count it to be any more than half-hardy. It is, however, a superb shrub for the cool greenhouse and can be kept in condition throughout the year if its flowering stems are cut back as soon as they show signs of running.

Both stems and leaves are white and densely felted and the latter are so delicately cut that they might well be made out of some exquisite lace. The plant itself is slow growing and can be kept in a 6″ pot for several years. Propagation can be either from seed or from cuttings. Seed sown in heat in February is usually ready to be pricked out into 3″ pots in March.

CONVOLVULUS *cneorum*

Origin:	Southern Europe, including Greece.
Habit:	Sub-shrub. Ht. 18″, allow 18″ width.
Hardiness:	4.
Use:	Border or rock garden.
Planting time:	May.
Main pruning:	After flowering.
Propagation:	Cuttings, root cuttings and layers.

It is somewhat surprising to find that this superb silver shrub should be a close relation of that pernicious weed bellbind for it has none of the evil habits of its relations and is, in fact, rather a difficult and very slow growing shrub.

There are some things in life worth persevering with and

98

Convolvulus cneorum is certainly one, for a good specimen is a proud sight, whether it be in flower or not. The individual leaves are heavily covered with a very fine silky down which catches the light and gives an impression of shimmering iridescence. In May, and sometimes in early September, the appearance of the plant changes completely, for every bit of silvery foliage disappears behind the terminal clusters of pink-throated white flowers. These keep going for about three to four weeks but do not seem to upset the balance of the plant for, once the old flowering stems have been cut back, the foliage immediately recovers its brilliance.

Convolvulus cneorum is really a scree plant and is always found in crevasses. It is therefore quite essential to see that its root is forced to go down for food and moisture. Young plants are usually potted into 3″ pots and must be surrounded with a lot of grit when they are put out. Some gardeners take out a hole 6″ deep and 6″ across and fill this with pure grit before planting, but in my experience it is safer to mix two parts of grit with one of soil so that one can plant firmly without leaving air-holes. Another way of persuading a young *Convolvulus cneorum* that it is being asked to grow in its native crevasse, is to set the young plant between two bricks stood up on end in the soil and fill the gap with soil and grit. Whichever method is adopted, the drainage below the plant must be perfect, for the roots cannot stand a cold, wet sub-soil.

Although a few bright sprigs of *Convolvulus cneorum* might well be the making of many an arrangement, the growth is so slow that it cannot be considered as a plant for cutting. Neither should it ever be over-pruned. Dead-heading after flowering is merely a matter of shortening back the stems by about 6″, whilst in May all that needs to be done is to remove any dead or tatty growth.

This is not an easy subject to increase though every now and again it is possible to find a runner which can be grown on independently, providing the connecting root has been severed some weeks before the young plant is lifted. Theoretically *Convolvulus cneorum* can be grown from root cuttings but these are almost impossible to find unless the whole plant is dug out and who would want to destroy an established specimen. Hard wood cuttings are sometimes successful when taken in August but must be left in situ for the winter and covered with a cloche. Tip-cuttings $1\frac{1}{2}$″ in length, taken in May, are easier to handle but they need bottom heat and take at least 6 weeks to root. During this time they run a grave risk of botrytis and must therefore be dusted with Orthocide every week. The best plants, however, are those raised from layers, which generally strike if pegged down in July.

CYNARA *cardunculus* (Cardoon)

Origin: Southern Europe.
Habit: Perennial. Ht. 5', allow 24" width and plant in groups of three.
Hardiness: 2.
Use: Back of border and for cutting.
Planting time: April.
Propagation: Seed.

Although the Cardoon was originally grown for the sake of its edible stems and ribs, these were taken from young plants, and involved as much work as the raising of celery. It is likely therefore that the plant would have disappeared from our gardens had it not been for the interest shown by flower decorators.

The foliage and habit are almost identical to those of the Globe Artichoke (*C. scolymus*) and there are many authorities who believe that they are in fact one and the same species, for the Artichoke has never been found growing wild.

As a decorative subject the Cardoon is probably a better choice than the Artichoke, for it is slightly larger and keeps its foliage in better condition in early autumn. It is true that its flower heads are not edible, but they dry well and make superb centres for winter decorations.

Cardoons need rich loam and do best when they can get their roots right down into the subsoil. In a county like Essex where the rainfall is always low in summer it is essential to mulch the roots in spring so as to conserve moisture. With the exception of some dead-heading, established plants need little attention till October when all old stems and dirty leaves must be cleared away. In this area it has not proved necessary to cover the stumps in winter but in the colder parts of the country they would probably appreciate the same sort of protection recommended for Artichokes.

Cardoon seed will germinate in the open if sown in a trench in

April, but as the seedlings are not very hardy many gardeners prefer sowing under glass in March and keeping the young plants in 3″ pots until it is safe to put them out in May.

Whether they should be put into their permanent quarters straight away, or into a nursery bed for one year is a matter of choice, but it must be remembered that Cardoons take at least three years to reach maturity, and that in their first year from seed they are unlikely to make more than rosettes of large silvery leaves. These leaves play an important part in the development of the plant, and must not be taken as cut foliage. Unfortunately they are quite beautiful and many a healthy young specimen has been stunted because somebody could not resist taking a leaf. When there is any danger of this happening it is just as well to grow a good reserve in the cutting border.

Fully established Cardoons are difficult to move as the main root goes straight down into the ground, but young stock can be lifted in October, by which time their leaves should have wilted.

The giant leaves, often 8″ across and a foot in length, are reasonably easy to harden once they are fully grown, but immature foliage is seldom reliable, and has a nasty habit of wilting the moment the weather turns hot. Failures with mature leaves are generally the result of carelessness at the time of cutting. The base of each stem must be got into water as soon as it is cut, and many experienced exhibitors go further and make doubly certain that the water can force its way into the leaves by recutting all the stems under water.

CYNARA *scolymus*

THE GLOBE ARTICHOKE

Origin:	North Africa.
Habit:	Perennial. Ht. 4′–5′. Plant in groups of three, 2′ apart.
Hardiness:	3.
Use:	For the back of the border and for cutting. Heads edible.
Planting time:	April.
Propagation:	Seeds and suckers.

There are so few bold foliaged silvers tall enough to stand at the back of the border that it seems strange that such a magnificent subject as the Globe Artichoke should ever be banished to the kitchen garden.

Perhaps if it did not produce those delicious heads for the gourmet the average gardener would be more inclined to appreciate the shape of the leaves and the beauty of the plant itself.

Although requiring sun and good drainage Artichokes are unlike most silvers in many ways for they need well manured ground, plenty of water in summer and some protection in winter. Most growers prepare the site in autumn by double digging and incorporating a liberal dressing of farmyard manure, but in my experience this is not absolutely essential and the plants do well in any well dug soil which has been enriched with a solid sea-weed manure such as Neptune's Bounty.

Established plants often carry a great number of heads at the same time but these never seem to affect the foliage provided they are removed before their scales start to open. This is of course the right moment to harvest them for the kitchen, but it often happens that too many heads mature at the same time so that some get left on the plant. This does nothing to improve either the heads or the leaves, for the former lose their flavour and the latter their vitality, and it should not be allowed to happen. The heads will keep in good condition for several days if they are cut with long stalks and put in water like flowers, and once they have been removed the leaves are safe.

Although the effects of cleaning up most silvers in autumn can be catastrophic, there is no question that the Globe Artichoke must be cut back to sound wood in October, for if the withered foliage and decayed stems are left to rot they become horribly slimy. This is also the time when the plants should be covered with straw or bracken held in place with a light coating of soil. This cover must not be removed till April for new suckers are often damaged by early spring frosts. Established plants appreciate having their roots mulched with garden compost, rotted manure or even straw before they start to grow, and it is important to do everything possible to conserve moisture. Even so Artichokes use a lot of water and they will probably need water at the first sign of drought, but it is better not to water them at all if they cannot be given a full ration of at least one and a half gallons per plant. Hoeing and fluffing up the composting material after watering will often make this dose last for ten days in hot weather.

Many flower decorators use the great leaves of the Artichoke for the large designs but although they are superbly shaped I have always found them inclined to be soft and unreliable, and cannot suggest a hardening technique which will succeed every time. It is obviously essential to find a mature leaf and to get the base of the stem into water the moment it is cut, but I believe that it is just as important to let the leaves stay in their hardening pails in a cool spot for at least twelve hours before using them. However, even this drill is not infallible, and for exhibition work I would always choose the leaves of the Onopordon in preference to those of the Artichoke. Slightly wilted leaves will sometimes respond to being stood in warm water, but nothing can be done once the whole leaf has become flabby.

Epicures will no doubt want to grow one of the French types such as Gros Vert de Laon. These named cultivars have to be propagated by sucker, but gardeners who are merely looking for border decoration will find that a packet of seed sown in heat in February, or in the open in April, will produce a quantity of plants some of which may well carry palatable heads.

Seedlings need to be chosen with care, for those with prickly leaves seldom produce good edible heads, whilst any that are green when young are unlikely to be silvery when mature.

Suckers are found at the side of old plants and can be removed in April with a strong sharp knife when 9″ high. It is important to leave some on the parent and to see that those taken have a piece of the old root attached. Suckers planted into their permanent quarters in April will usually produce a few heads in their first season, but do not reach their full height for another year.

DIANTHUS HYBRIDS

Origin: Garden.
Habit: Perennial. Mat or cushion. Ht. 4–12″, allow 6–12″ width.
Hardiness: 2.
Use: Border.
Planting time: August–October. March–April.
Propagation: Layers and cuttings.

So many of the Dianthus have lovely flowers that it is easy to forget that some make perfect cushions of grey-blue foliage and retain their colour just as well in winter as they do in summer.

It would be impossible to mention all the varieties and cultivars to which this applies, but the hardy hybrid pink known as 'Pink Bouquet' must surely be one of the best, for it always makes a perfect round cushion of cheerful grey-blue foliage which it smothers with sugar-pink flowers in June, and again in September.

Some of the miniature and alpine pinks keep the colour of their foliage in the same way but tend to spread out into a mat rather than forming a cushion. One of the best of these is 'Crimson Treasure' which covers the ground with a carpet of grey-blue some 2″ deep. In summer it is seldom found without a few little crimson flowers, but it is in the depth of winter, when everything is looking tired, that this little plant is such a boon, for it always gives the impression of being ready to greet the spring.

Hybrid pinks grow best in a fertile soil which has been lightly enriched with some organic food such as well made garden compost, spent mushroom compost or hop manure. This must not be buried as the whole of the genus *Dianthus* is surface-rooting, and prefers to find its food in the top 4″ of soil. The alpines and miniatures, on the other hand, suffer if the ground on which they are growing is too rich, and usually do best when planted in perfectly ordinary well drained garden soil.

Pinks are supposed to be lime-loving, but in my experience these modern Pinks do not want a surfeit of lime, and certainly do not require all the lime mortar they are so often given. I grow them in a neutral soil with a pH of 6·5 and would certainly not think of giving them extra unless the pH dropped to under 6. When lime is needed a couple of handfuls of limestone chippings per plant at planting time should suffice, and this again merely needs mixing with the top four inches of soil.

Many failures with hybrid pinks are due to root scorch, and though 'Pink Bouquet', the cultivar mentioned above, is tougher than most, it will always do better if its roots are shaded from the heat of the sun by some creeping plant such as *Artemisia lanata pedemontana*.

Pinks are usually propagated by cuttings, but the two cultivars mentioned can be layered in July and this is a great deal less troublesome. The layers are best left in situ for the winter, but can be moved if necessary in March.

The bare stems of pinks that have just been pegged down are not attractive, and this often discourages layering in the border. It is, however, possible to cover these ugly stems by planting something else right up against the root of the parent pink. I have tried *Helichrysum petiolatum* and *Artemisia schmidtiana*. The former grew too fast and nearly smothered the layers, but a specially grown specimen of *Artemisia schmidtiana*, propagated in March and kept in a 4½″ pot, seemed the perfect answer, for its shoots were just long enough to hide the bare stems of the pink in July, and died off in October when they were no longer needed. Furthermore, in the following year, the whole group looked as though it had been laid out intentionally. *Artemisia schmidtiana* would, of course, swamp any of the miniature pinks, but *Artemisia glacialis* is just about the right size and can be used in the same way.

EUCALYPTUS *gunnii*

Origin:	Tasmania.
Habit:	Upright tree. Ht. 50′, allow 4′ width when grown as a bush.
Hardiness:	3–4.
Use:	As background.
Planting time:	May.
Main pruning:	May.
Propagation:	Seed.

For many years, while gardeners in the South have been regarding gums of all kinds as delicate, those on the East coast of Scotland have been experimenting and there are now a number of established trees in Fife which prove that several species are reasonably hardy. Of these, *gunnii* is certainly one of the toughest and at the same time, one of the most useful.

It was an old gardener in Fife who warned me always to protect the trunk of all gums, for he had learnt that his trees only died when this was cracked in a hard frost. He used the old-fashioned straw covers which used to be used to protect wine bottles, but a few bunches of straw, wound round the trunk and held together with bass, serve the same purpose.

The snag with all gums is that they are forest trees and really too big for most gardens. They also have two kinds of leaves, juvenile which are rounded and adult which are pointed. It is the juvenile leaves which are the most attractive but these disappear as the tree grows upwards.

For the past five years I have been experimenting with a tree which I am growing as a bush. When this was about 5' tall its top was cut out leaving 3'. Side branches are cut back as they grow and used as material for flower arrangements. So far, the foliage which is carried by the young breaks is always rounded, but whether this will continue much longer is a different matter.

Eucalyptus branches make lovely decorations and need no special hardening drill, but they consume an incredible amount of water and often need topping up twice a day.

Gums cannot be grown from cuttings but germinate easily if sown in mild heat in February. Many growers refrigerate their seed in the cold box in the refrigerator for about a fortnight before sowing. The seedlings are ready to prick out into pots as soon as they start to show their first leaves. These seedlings vary and some are a lot more glaucous than others so it is always wise to pot up a few spares in order to be able to select the best.

EURYOPS *acraeus*

(*Euryops evansii*)

Origin:	Drakensburg, South Africa.
Habit:	Shrub. Ht. 12″, allow 18″ width.
Hardiness:	2.
Use:	Border. Rockery.
Planting time:	April–May, and September on light land.
Main pruning:	After flowering.
Propagation:	Layers. Cuttings.

A tidy little grey-blue shrub which keeps its foliage throughout the winter and can stand any amount of frost; should be the perfect choice for rockeries and borders, and this was so for many years, but recently *Euryops* has become the victim of a pernicious form of rust which seems to be resistant to all fungicides. Efforts are being made to bring in a new strain from South Africa and at the same time to find a cure for the fungus, but until some progress has been made, *Euryops acraeus* is not a subject to recommend.

This is a tragedy, for it was pleasant to look out on a grim day in winter and see a little patch of pale grey-blue, whilst in May the flower crop of clear yellow flowers was quite one of the sights of the border. These flowers, incidentally, were so numerous that they had to be dead-headed with shears.

For those who can get hold of a clean strain, it should be said that it can be layered in summer or increased by small cuttings found at the base of the flowering stems. These need to be about 2″ long and will root without heat if planted in July.

FESTUCA *ovina glauca*

Origin:	Britain and other cool countries.
Habit:	Tufted perennial. Ht. 6″, allow 7″ width.
Hardiness:	1.
Use:	Edges of border.
Planting time:	March–October, November.
Propagation:	Division.

Gardeners are inclined to neglect grasses but there are very few edging plants suitable for all kinds of soil which will remain tidier than this little Festuca with its grey-blue foliage. It pays to try to remove the flowering stems for they are straw coloured and do nothing to improve the blue effect. Otherwise, no special attention is needed and though the plants may appear somewhat sad in winter, they come to life quite early in spring and remain attractive throughout the summer and autumn.

Propagation is by division, preferably in autumn and, though this is a plant which divides easily enough, it is unwise to be greedy and try to make too many plants out of one parent, for every piece needs to be at least an inch in diameter if it is to succeed.

GAZANIA 'Silver Beauty'

Origin:	Garden.
Habit:	Spreading perennial. Ht. 6″, allow 12″ width.
Hardiness:	6.

Use: Bedding and as a temporary ground-cover.
Planting time: May.
Propagation: Cuttings.

There are many grey and white leaved Gazanias but this seems to be the whitest of all and it has the additional virtue of being a very fast grower, which is important in a plant which is only half-hardy.

The flowers of all Gazanias close when the sun goes in, and I doubt whether anyone would grow 'Silver Beauty' for the sake of its yellow and black flowers, but its leaves are beautifully formed and might well have been cut out of a piece of the palest grey velvet. Furthermore, as these leaves are heavily felted from the start the impression given by 'Silver Beauty' is always reminiscent of the newly washed shirt in the T.V. commercial!

Although I would never like to suggest that 'Silver Beauty' was in any way hardy it should, I think, be recorded that Mrs. Scott Montcrieff kept a magnificent specimen for many years in her cold garden in Suffolk, and merely covered its centre with a cloche in winter, leaving the sprawling shoots to wither in the frost. Whether this would work everywhere is doubtful, for I must confess that this particular plant stood on the very top of a steep bank.

It is debatable whether it is better to house old plants in October or to rely on August rooted cuttings. The old plants, when lifted, make quite attractive pot-plants which stay in condition for about a month in a sitting-room. If, at the end of this time, they are cut back and left to rest in a cool greenhouse, they will recover in time for planting in May, when they should spread out over four square feet.

Plenty of cuttings can be found in August and they will root readily in sand but the young plants must always be grown on in a frost-proof greenhouse.

GLAUCIUM *flavum*

and

GLAUCIUM *corniculatum* (*phoenicium*)

Origin: Europe.
Habit: Monocarpic. Foliage 8″ to 9″ tall. Allow 8″ width.
Hardiness: 1.

Use: Front of Border.
Planting time: April.
Propagation: Seed.

The foliage of these two Horned Poppies is almost identical, that of *corniculatum* being perhaps slightly more curly and having a reddish tinge to the base of the leaves. Their habit and the treatment they require is identical, and, as they cross-fertilise very easily, there are a great many hybrids about.

According to most experts *Glaucium flavum* is sometimes perennial and *Glaucium corniculatum* definitely annual, but in my experience, both will die if allowed to set seed but will live for many years if grown purely as foliage plants. The flowers, incidentally, are different, *Glaucium flavum* being yellow and those of *corniculatum* orange-red.

As foliage plants they are well entitled to a position in any garden, for their 8″ to 9″ long leaves are a good silver and superbly formed. Both species, however, have a persistent urge to flower and will produce the occasional flowering stem at any time of year. These must, of course, be cut out when young.

For cutting, the leaves of these Glauciums are without equal for the heart of medium-sized designs. They keep well and can be found with good stems but must be handled with care for they are inclined to be brittle.

Seed should be sown in March and it is important to pot the seedlings into 2″ or 3″ pots before they show their first true leaves. At this stage the root of the seedling will be nothing more than a thread and it will not notice the move. This is important for Glauciums will not stand having their roots broken. It is true that at first these tiny seedlings will seem lost in their pots, but if they are kept going with a spray for the first week or so they will soon fill out and should be ready for the open border in late April.

HELICHRYSUM *angustifolium*

Origin: Eastern United States.
Habit: Shrub. Ht. 2′, allow 2′ width.
Hardiness: 3.
Use: Border. Front of shrubbery. Ground cover.
Planting time: April–May.

Main pruning: May.
Propagation: Cuttings and layers.

If marks could be given to shrubs in accordance with their appearance throughout the year, *Helichrysum angustifolium* would be certain to come out at the top of the list, for its foliage is always bright silver in spring and summer and loses very little of its lustre in winter.

The leaves, small and almost needle-like, are densely packed round each shoot and only lose their silvery appearance when the shoot is running up to flower. The flowers, which come in flat terminal clusters, are not a very pleasant yellow and do nothing for the border. Thus it seems better to put the shears over the plant as soon as the little silver stems start to elongate. This serves not only to prevent flowering, but also to produce a fresh crop of young shoots.

The leaves of many Helichrysums have a faint smell of curry, but in *angustifolium* this smell is very pronounced and is inclined to waft through the garden. Some may like it, but even those who do not would be well advised not to refuse this plant a place, for it is probably one of the most reliable of all silver shrubs.

Soft wood cuttings can be struck on bottom heat at practically any time of the year, but if no bottom heat is available it is better to wait for semi-hard cuttings in July. These are usually about 5″ long and should be taken from non-flowering stems. They root quicker when taken with a heel.

HELICHRYSUM *fontanesii*

Origin: Sicily.
Habit: Shrub. Ht. 4′, allow 30″ width.
Hardiness: 3.
Use: Border and shrubbery.
Planting time: May.
Main pruning: May.
Propagation: Layers and cuttings.

When a special site needs a bold white-leaved bush there is nothing more effective than *Helichrysum fontanesii*, a plant which can be grown with a minimum of effort. The leaves of well-established specimens are only about $\frac{1}{4}$″ wide, but at least 4″ long and so heavily felted in summer that they seem almost white. The pale yellow flowers which are carried in flat terminal clusters are of moderate value. They are not ugly, but whether they are worth leaving is a matter of opinion, for the plants show signs of losing their vigour from the moment the stems start to run. This can be proved if one specimen is allowed to flower and the young stems of another are cut back before they even show buds, for it will take five or six weeks for the first plant to recover from dead-heading but countless fresh breaks will appear on the second within a week of shearing.

Helichrysum fontanesii makes a big effort to retain its foliage throughout the winter but it must be admitted that the result is not very attractive and that most gardeners look forward to cutting away the dirty shoots in early May. How much growth to remove must depend on whether the plant concerned can be allowed to fill a larger space than it did in the previous year, but hard pruning of this species does not lead to a pretty shape. Young plants, however, cannot be allowed to straggle and their side shoots need stopping regularly.

It is usually possible to find some stems that can be brought down on to the ground and layered, but semi-hard cuttings are perfectly easy to find in July and will root quickly if taken with a heel. The young plants are tolerably hardy.

HELICHRYSUM *italicum*

Origin:	Southern Europe.
Habit:	Shrub. Ht. 12″–18″, allow 12″ width.
Hardiness:	4.
Use:	For very low hedges.
Planting time:	May.
Main pruning:	May.
Propagation:	Cuttings.

The only value of this little shrub is as a substitute for Box for it clips well and will grow into delightful baby hedges if trimmed in May and July. Unfortunately, however, *Helichrysum italicum* does demand very sharp drainage and will not overwinter unless grown on either sand or gravel.

As an ordinary garden plant it is always inferior to *Helichrysum angustifolium* and not nearly as silvery.

Propagation is easy from July cuttings but young plants are completely allergic to frost and must be housed for the winter.

HELICHRYSUM *marginatum*

Origin:	South Africa.
Habit:	Hummock forming. Ht. 6″, allow 8″ width.
Hardiness:	3.
Use:	Rockery.
Planting time:	May.
Propagation:	Rooted offshoots.

It is hard to discover just what this Helichrysum does require, for though it will not establish itself in this Colchester area, it does well when planted on a well drained soil both in Jersey and in Cumberland.

Certainly it is a plant to covet, for its tiny rosettes of white leaves build up to form a lovely solid mole-hill which keeps clean throughout the summer. The pretty little russet pink everlasting flowers are carried on 4″ stems and open from pink buds. They are greatly treasured but do not appear every year.

It is not an easy subject to root from a cutting but it is often possible to detach a rosette, complete with root, from the edge of a clump, and if this is either potted or planted in well drained soil it should take hold. The only trouble is that in this area the wretched thing remains as a single rosette. Perhaps this is because *Helichrysum marginatum* is the one silver which does not appreciate a constant easterly wind.

PLATE III

1   Helichrysum fontanesii
2   Helichrysum petiolatum
3   Glaucum phoenicium (including basal leaves)
4   Convolvulus cneorum

HELICHRYSUM *petiolatum*

Origin:	Australia.
Habit:	Spreading perennial. Allow 18″ width.
Hardiness:	6.
Use:	As temporary ground cover or for trailing.
Planting time:	Late May.
Propagation:	Cuttings.

There are very few borders so perfectly planned that they never show a bare patch of earth and it is sometimes useful to know of a plant which can be put out late in May with the knowledge that it will stretch out over a square foot within a month. The only trouble with *Helichrysum petiolatum* is that it tends to grow too fast and to smother everything if its lovely curving sprays of foliage are not drastically cut back in August.

The individual leaves are heart-shaped and a mere ½″ in length. They are not actually grey but rather pale green covered with a very short white pile. The general effect of a plant is certainly white rather than silver, but the charm probably lies in the arching habit of the branches which always curve towards the ground. Although some energetic gardeners are prepared to grow a few plants up stakes, I have never thought that the results were worth the effort. On the other hand, the contrast between the grey of *Helichrysum petiolatum* and the shiny evergreen leaves of *Caenothus dentatus* is worth remembering and it is not difficult to encourage a few sprays to intermingle with any wall shrub.

Helichrysum petiolatum is often seen in hanging baskets or draped over walls, and it is a most accommodating plant which can be trained to cover almost anything. It has a remarkably small root in comparison with the spread of its branches and will thrive when planted in quite a tiny pocket.

Plants grown out of doors seldom have time to flower, but when the tips of shoots on glasshouse specimens start to lengthen it can be assumed that they are trying to run to bud and need removing. The flower heads have no real decorative value and are mere clusters of biscuit coloured papery florets set on bare stalks. Luckily the flowering period does not last for long and on well grown specimens the majority of sprays make no attempt to 'run'. Hence 'cutting-back' is not a tedious chore.

Although *Helichrysum petiolatum* is useful for cutting, immature shoots can be very unreliable and it is as well not to trust a piece unless it is well covered with small side shoots. These start as extra small leaves growing from the upper side of the stem. Mature pieces will always show a few of these spare leaves within a few inches of the tip. Hardening consists of scraping the base of the stem and putting this into very hot water.

As to propagation, if six 4″ cuttings are planted in a 6″ pot containing sand and compost in August, and this is placed in a sunless window indoors, the roots should appear within three weeks. The foliage must, of course, be kept turgid with regular spraying. At the end of this time the cuttings can be treated as growing plants and kept in the full light. This is difficult without a glasshouse but much can be achieved if a pot is stood in a sunny window and turned daily. If all is well the young plants will start to show new growth in February and will need stopping in March. Potting into individual pots can be delayed till early April, which gives the roots enough time to recover from being separated.

Gardeners with glass will be well advised to lift the plant in September and take 3″ cuttings in February or March. They grow so quickly that there is no need to be in too much of a hurry, for well developed plants in 3″ pots need a lot of attention and water.

HELICHRYSUM *plicatum*

Origin:	South-eastern Europe.
Habit:	Bushy shrub. Ht. 2′, allow 20″ width.
Hardiness:	3.
Use:	Border.
Planting time:	April–May.
Main pruning:	May.
Propagation:	Cuttings in July. Layering.

This might be described as a smaller version of *Helichrysum fontanesii* for it grows into much the same kind of round bush and has slightly smaller leaves which are of much the same shape. From a distance, however, there is a considerable difference in colour between the two species for while *Helichrysum fontanesii* is virtually white, the foliage of *Helichrysum plicatum* shows a distinct tinge of pale green.

The terminal clusters of yellow flowers have no particular beauty and, if the flowering stems can be cut away before they form buds, the foliage remains in better condition throughout summer and autumn. *Helichrysum plicatum* keeps its leaves throughout the winter, but they lose their lustre at the first sign of hard weather.

Propagation can either be by layers or cuttings. The latter are quite easy to find, for every stem carries quantities of side breaks which can be taken with a heel in July. No heat is needed at this time, but soft early spring cuttings will not root without bottom heat.

HELICHRYSUM *plicatum* 'Elmstead'

Origin:	Garden.
Habit:	Bushy shrub. Ht. 2', allow 20" width.
Hardiness:	2.
Use:	Border shrub.
Planting time:	April–May.
Main pruning:	May.
Propagation:	Layers and cuttings.

Many good garden plants have been raised from stray seedlings and one of the greatest thrills is to come upon a self-sown seedling and realise that it is superior to its parent.

In 1958 one such seedling appeared under an old plant of *Helichrysum plicatum*. At the time it seemed that its foliage was bolder than that of its parent and so it was carefully lifted and grown on. Just before the hard winter, rooted plants were sent to various parts of the country for trial. One of the gardens selected was a very difficult one in Suffolk which lay in a notorious frost pocket. The bitter winter proved too much for most of the silvers in this particular garden. As these included hardy subjects such as *Santolina serratifolia* it was surprising to find that the Helichrysum on trial had come through unscathed although a well established specimen of *Helichrysum plicatum* had succumbed. Further tests have proved that this was no mere fluke.

It may be that the original plant was not merely a *Helichrysum plicatum* seedling but the result of a cross between this and

Helichrysum splendidum. Certainly there was a specimen of the latter standing quite close to the seed parent and undoubtedly *splendidum* is the toughest of all the Helichrysums.

Be this as it may, *Helichrysum plicatum* 'Elmstead' is undoubtedly a very good plant, worthy of a position in any border and quite invaluable for those who cannot grow a large selection of silvers. It should, of course, be treated in exactly the same way as *Helichrysum plicatum*.

HELICHRYSUM *splendidum*

Origin:	South Africa.
Habit:	Bushy shrub. Ht. 2', allow 18".
Hardiness:	1.
Use:	Border.
Planting time:	April.
Main pruning:	April.
Propagation:	Heel cuttings.

If this Helichrysum was easier to keep in apple-pie condition it would be quite invaluable, for it will grow in cold, damp spots which would daunt most silvers.

The foliage is a good silver and the little leaves are velvety but the shrub itself is inclined to become terribly leggy and it is seldom that one finds a stem that does not carry quite a number of withered leaves amongst the young ones. If the dead leaves would only fall off this might not be too bad, but they hang on in a most determined manner and spoil the whole effect.

Drastic pruning in April and shearing in early July goes some way towards helping both foliage and shape, but shrubs that have been treated in this manner take several years to grow up to their proper height.

The insignificant little yellow daisies are carried on short, stubby stems and may appear at any time of the year, including February. They are best dead-headed with shears.

The growth that comes through from April pruning seldom flowers much before the end of June. By that time the foliage is getting very tatty and needs to be replaced by fresh growth. This is the time to use shears again for it is not necessary to cut deep into the plant but rather merely to remove the top few inches of each and every stem. This treatment leaves the plant looking very bare for a while but it does ensure a reasonable display of foliage throughout the rest of the year.

Like most Helichrysums, *splendidum* will root from heel cuttings taken in July. These can be set in a sandy compost in the garden and merely need to be covered with a cloche. Young plants are extremely hardy and can be left in situ.

LAVENDULA *lanata*

Origin: Spain.
Habit: Small shrub. Ht. 12"–18", allow 12" width.
Hardiness: 4.
Use: Border and greenhouse.
Planting time: May.
Main pruning: After flowering.
Propagation: Seed sown under glass in March.

This little shrub is, unfortunately, not an easy one to grow but it does survive in gardens which, for some reason or other, are too dry for most subjects. Thus, it has established itself very happily in a garden in Norfolk which stands on the top of a hill and is full of conifer roots, whilst in mid-Essex there is a magnificent specimen clinging to the very edge of a gravel pit.

The flower of *Lavendula lanata* is almost violet but, though it is slightly scented, the real scent comes from the leaves which fill the air with their fragrance every time they are touched.

This shrub never grows to any size nor does it ever become untidy. If the flowering stems are cut out carefully, there should be no need for any further pruning but it does improve the appearance if some of the old foliage is cut away in May.

Lavendula lanata does not root easily from cuttings but can be grown quite easily from seed.

LAVENDULA *spica* 'The Dutch Lavender'

Origin: Garden.
Habit: Bushy shrub. Ht. 2' 6", allow 20" width.

Hardiness: 2.
Use: Border. Low Hedge.
Planting time: April.
Main pruning: After flowering.
Propagation: Semi-mature cuttings in August.

Most forms of *Lavendula spica* are inclined to look somewhat drab when planted amongst true silvers but this does not apply to the Dutch Lavender which has quite clean grey foliage. Nor are its flowers without scent for this is one of the varieties of *Lavendula spica* grown for oil. The Dutch Lavender is slightly smaller than the English Lavender and makes a good hedge which keeps very tidy.

This Lavender roots readily from 3″ cuttings taken with a heel in August or September. These will strike if set in a sandy compost in the garden and covered. The heel is important as without it the chance of striking the cutting is halved.

LEUCANTHEMUM *hosmarense*
(*Chrysanthemum hosmariense* or *C. maresii* var. *hosmariensis*)

Origin: Morocco.
Habit: Bushy shrublet. Ht. 9″, allow 12″ width.
Hardiness: 2.
Use: Border or rock garden.
Planting time: April–May.
Main pruning: April.
Propagation: Cuttings.

This is a true plant for all seasons, for it keeps its finely cut steel-blue foliage in remarkably good condition throughout the winter and has a delightful habit of producing bold white marguerite-like flowers at any time of year, including winter, although the real flowering season comes in May.

It makes a tidy little bush and seems content to flourish on neglect, but it cannot be said to be a plant for cutting for it is seldom possible to find a flower or a sprig with a decent stem.

The removal of a large number of cuttings is inclined to spoil the appearance of the plant and when a number of cuttings are required, it is really better to use one specimen as a potential parent and to cut it back to within 6″ of the ground in June. This will result in a superb crop of breaks which can be taken as soon as they are 3″ long and have produced their first four leaves. These will root without heat if placed in a sandy mixture. The young plants are tolerably hardy and will overwinter in the garden if planted in a well drained position.

ONOPORDON *arabicum*

Origin:	Southern Europe.
Habit:	Monocarpic, usually biennial. Ht. 7′–8′, allow 18″ width.
Hardiness:	1.
Use:	Back of border.
Planting time:	September–October.
Propagation:	Seed.

There will, I suppose, always be an argument as to whether this or *Onopordon acantheum* was the original thistle brought back from the Holy Land by the Crusaders and eventually adopted as the emblem of Scotland, but the argument is becoming somewhat academic, for the two species have virtually merged and it is now impossible to find a true strain of *Onopordon acantheum* (which should never grow to more than 5′).

Onopordons can be used at the back of summer borders and look magnificent when planted near a group of stately *Verbascum bombicyferum* spires. Their stems are nearly white and their leaves silvery. When first planted they concentrate on lengthening out a cluster of beautifully designed leaves. In June the flowering stem emerges from this rosette and proceeds to grow at the rate of a foot a week. As the main stem grows, so side branches appear until each plant measures 7′ or 8′ in height and probably covers a square yard. These side-shoots will intertwine if the plants are planted in groups 18″ apart, and this is the only way I know of growing Onopordons without stakes, for single plants always get blown over. The thistle heads start to show in late July and run to seed within a fortnight. The entire plant collapses if the seed-heads are left to mature, but will last for the whole autumn if dead-headed. Onopordons are incredibly prickly and the spines which grow on the edge of their leaves can cause minor poisoning. A clump of Onopordon makes a magnificent barrier and will go a long way towards discouraging the use of a forbidden path.

Flower decorators can find endless uses for the leaves of Onopordon, which keeps astoundingly well in water and need no special hardening. It is only the leaves of young plants which can be used in this manner for those growing up the stem of flowering specimens are short and have no proper stems. Side branches take water well, but when an entire plant is needed for mammoth decorations it is essential to fill the hollow stem with water and plug it with cotton wool before placing it in a bucket. As Onopordons are very big, this often means climbing up on to a ladder!

Onopordons are raised from seed which will germinate at any time of year if it is soaked for an hour before being sown. Plants intended for the border can be planted in the open in July and transplanted in October. This is also the time to look round for self-sown seedlings for, though this thistle has never been known to make a nuisance of itself, seedlings can be difficult to move if they are left to grow up amongst the small plants. For a constant supply of leaves a small amount of seed should be set at fortnightly intervals from March onwards.

ROMNEYA *coulteri*
(The Californian Bush Poppy)

Origin:	California.
Habit:	Bushy shrub. Ht. 5′, allow for a spread of not more than 18″ in second year but up to 4′ thereafter.
Use:	Back of border. Wall shrub.
Hardiness:	3.
Planting time:	April.
Main pruning:	April.
Propagation:	Division in April. Root cuttings in September or from off-sets.

Gardeners often grumble that there are so few tall silver shrubs, but forget that the foliage of the Californian Bush Poppy is glaucous, and that it is an outstanding shrub which deserves a position of honour in every collection of grey-foliaged plants.

The large, scented, poppy-like flowers, with their golden centres and pure white petals, start to open towards the end of August, and at this time of year a good bush is certainly a memorable sight. Most garden specimens are probably grown for the sake of their superb poppies, but the foliage of a Romneya is not without decorative value and the shrub is very attractive even when not in flower.

Romneyas require much the same conditions as true silvers, but dislike wind and a soil that has become impoverished. How much organic manure should be forked in before planting is impossible to define, but I would suggest that they be given half the amount that would be required by a rose. Top dressing is seldom necessary or wise, for though overfeeding may promote growth, it certainly inhibits the production of flowers. Nobody should ever expect to be able to establish a Romneya very quickly and to do this may take more than three years, but once the plant has settled down it is there for ever and may even try to take over the entire border if its roots are not contained.

Mature foliage will stand quite well in water if the bases of the stems are singed, but it is the gorgeous flowers which most decorators covet and it is useful to know that these will keep superbly when cut at the cracking bud stage and allowed to open in water.

Propagation can either be by division in April or from root cuttings taken in September. Division seems like vandalism to me, for once a plant has become established, it is wrong to disturb it. The second method, on the other hand, is none too reliable, even though it is always possible to find suitable thongs round every old plant. Luckily the wandering roots of an established specimen tend to throw up a shoot from time to time. These shoots may appear at some distance from the main stool and can be grown into good plants, providing they are not lifted until they have made their own independent root system which they do not start to do until the root connecting them with the parent shrub has been severed. Quite a number of plants can be made in this way, and it is certainly the easiest and kindest method of increasing a somewhat stubborn subject.

SALVIA *argentea*

Origin: Mediterranean.
Habit: Monocarpic. Flowering stem 4′, allow 14″.
Hardiness: 3.
Use: Front of border.
Planting time: April.
Propagation: Seed.

It seems sad that a plant that is capable of producing such lovely leaves as *Salvia argentea* should have such an ugly flowering spike. If only the leaves and stem were as white and woolly as the leaves at the base, this would indeed be a magnificent plant for the back of the border.

It must, however, be acknowledged that *Salvia argentea* cannot be considered as either grey or silver when in flower and that it is only worth growing for the sake of its silky basal leaves. But how lovely these big leaves are, sometimes 8″ in length and 6″ across and always well covered with silky hair, they seem so exotic that it is hard to realise that they belong to a perfectly hardy plant.

The art of growing this Salvia lies in catching the flowering growth before it has had a chance to run, and in removing all old leaves as soon as they show signs of turning green. These big old fellows spoil the appearance of the plant and at the same time shade the younger leaves so that they are unable to produce their cover of silk. The first flowering stem pushes itself up from the centre of the plant and is quite easy to spot. Subsequent stems have a tiresome habit of growing up under big leaves and often get overlooked until they are fairly big. This does not improve the appearance of the plant but does little permanent damage, for though *Salvia argentea* is officially classified as biennial, it seems capable of carrying a small crop of seed without trouble. *Salvia argentea* can often be used to give weight to the front edge of a border. Most of the low growing silvers, such as *Artemisia lanata pedemontana*, are light and lacy in texture and need the contrast of something solid.

Enthusiastic flower decorators are always tempted by the superb texture of these leaves, but often get sadly disappointed for they are not exactly reliable and often droop some hours after they have been put in water. Unfortunately, it often happens that the older leaves are rejected because of their short stems whilst others, pushing their way up behind older leaves, are chosen because they have longer stems regardless of the fact that they are still completely soft! These light-starved leaves can always be recognised by their green stems and soft tips.

Seedlings grow fast and a March sowing under glass will produce good plants in time for putting out in early May. Outside, the seed is best sown in summer, but slugs are particularly fond of the seedlings and they must be protected with cinders.

SANTOLINA *chamaecyparissus*
(*S. incana*)

Origin:	Southern Europe.
Habit:	Bushy shrub. Ht. 2′, allow 24″ width.
Hardiness:	1.
Use:	Border. Low hedge. Ground cover.
Planting time:	April–May.
Main pruning:	April.
Propagation:	Layering. Cuttings.

If one considers winter appearance this, the true Lavender Cotton, is a very underrated plant, probably because it is normally neglected and allowed to become woody.

Although capable of breaking from wood, it does not do so very freely and plants that have been drastically pruned seldom regain their shape, so it is better to prune gently every year in April and shorten back some of the foliage with shears when dead-heading in late July.

This treatment will keep a bush well rounded and there should not be any nasty gaps in the foliage. These can, however, be forced open by the strength of the flowering heads which is one good reason for removing all stems as soon as they are seen, the other being that the egg-yolk yellow flowers have no particular beauty. In spring the first growth is green but this changes very quickly and by early June both stems and leaves are heavily coated with wool. The serrated leaves are very narrow and only about 1″ long but they are so densely packed that the general appearance of the bush is silvery. Unfortunately, however, when the pieces are cut and brought indoors they are not very exciting and this is not a plant I would grow for cutting.

Santolina chamaecyparissus is easy enough to increase either by cuttings or by layers. Cuttings root best when they are semi-mature in August and have been taken with a heel. Layers can really be pegged down at any time of year for they never seem to notice that they have been partially detached from their parent. Whichever method is used, it pays to keep the plant very bushy while young and to keep on stopping it back. This treatment does much to prevent legginess.

SANTOLINA *chamaecyparissus nana*

(*S. incana nana*)

Origin:	Southern Europe.
Habit:	Bushy shrub. Ht. 12"–18", allow 18" width.
Hardiness:	3.
Use:	Border. Rock garden.
Planting time:	May.
Propagation:	Tip cuttings.

In many ways this is a miniature form of *Santolina chamaecyparissus* with shorter leaves and smaller flowers but there is one big difference, for the foliage of this little shrub, which looks so innocent, has the most pungent smell I know. Everyone has their own idea about scents and smells and there are those who do not dislike this particular smell but to some *Santolina chamaecyparissus nana* is a thoroughly undesirable plant.

Nevertheless, this variety is compact and tidy and keeps its foliage well in winter. It is very slow growing and needs little pruning, although all flowering stems are best removed while the flowers are still in bud.

It is sometimes difficult to strike from semi-mature wood but tip cuttings, about 1" in length, will root very quickly on bottom heat in November. These little cuttings are really the side-breaks found growing up the stems.

SANTOLINA *chamaecyparissus*

Origin:	Garden.
Habit:	Spreading shrub. Ht. 12″, allow 18″ width.
Hardiness:	3.
Use:	Front of border. Rock garden.
Planting time:	April–May.
Propagation:	Layering. Cuttings.

If *S. c. nana* is a *miniature* version of *Santolina chamaecyparissus*, 'Weston' is best described as a *dwarf* version of it, for its leaves and flowers are almost identical in size with those of the species, though it has a spreading, rather than an upright habit.

It is a very good plant and so white in summer that, from a distance, it often looks like a lump of cotton wool. Even more important, the foliage has no unpleasant smell.

Although this Santolina is by nature tidy, it is not improved by gaps left in the foliage after the flowering stems have forced themselves up from the base. This can be prevented if the stems are removed while they are still soft and pliable, in other words before the egg-yolk yellow flowers have actually opened.

Santolina 'Weston' will sometimes strike from a semi-mature cutting taken with a heel in July, but it is safer to take tip cuttings about 1½″ in November and root them on bottom heat. Layers can be pegged down in summer or autumn.

SANTOLINA *neapolitana*
(*S. rosmarinifolia*)

Origin:	Southern Italy. Spain. Portugal.
Habit:	Upright shrub. Ht. 2′, allow 2′ width.
Hardiness:	2.
Use:	Shrubbery.
Planting time:	April.
Main pruning:	After flowering.
Propagation:	Cuttings.

Although the foliage of this Santolina can at certain times be extremely silvery, I would query whether it should really be considered a grey, for both its young shoots and its flowering stems are bright green and in a wet season even the mature foliage is inclined to find it difficult to turn grey.

Furthermore, the pale lime-yellow flowers are produced in such quantities that they hide every bit of foliage for about a month. A bush of *Santolina neapolitana* in flower is a lovely sight but one which I would prefer seeing from a distance, for the smell of sulphur given off by the flowers can be overpowering.

However, it is a very graceful bush and, though its leaves are nearly as closely packed as those of *Santolina chamaecyparissus* and just as deeply cut, they are much longer and therefore look much lighter.

There are not many grey or silver shrubs which will tolerate being cut in autumn, but this Santolina is so hardy that it does not seem to mind losing a few pieces in October or November. These will keep well if hardened in hot water but need quite a lot of grooming before they are used. Although the old leaves wither away when their time comes, they never drop but stay attached to the undersides of the young leaves.

There must be some exceptions to all rules and I believe that it is better to prune this Santolina hard after flowering and merely to cut out dead and weak growth in spring. It is, in any case, so floriferous that, by the time all the flowering stems have been cut away, there is little left, and though pruning in July means a bare stump early in August, it does encourage a superb crop of foliage for the winter.

This particular Santolina strikes so easily from semi-mature cuttings taken with a heel in July and covered with a bell-glass or jar that it would be a waste of good glasshouse space to worry about any other form of propagation. Young plants develop sound wood very quickly and can just survive the winter without protection, but there is some evidence that they prefer being lightly covered, for plants that have been protected with a cloche always make the best specimens.

Santolinas need a lot of training in their first year and it would be inadvisable to allow a young *Santolina neapolitana* to go to flower too soon. Frequent stopping will prevent this and make the plant bushy.

SANTOLINA *neapolitana* var. *serratifolia*

Origin: Unknown.
Habit: Upright shrub. Ht. 2′, allow 18″.
Hardiness: 2.
Use: Border.
Planting time: April.
Main pruning: April.
Propagation: Cuttings.

Although the foliage of this variety is almost identical to that of *Santolina neapolitana*, there are some marked differences between the two plants. As a silver foliage plant this is probably the better for it does not flower so freely and therefore has more energy left for its foliage. It is true that as with *S. neapolitana* the young shoots and flowering stems of this Santolina are bright green, but the finely cut leaves turn silver as soon as they have had a few days' sun and, once the green stems have been cut out, the shrub becomes a very graceful silvery bush. The flower of *Santolina neapolitana* var. *serratifolia* is similar to that of *Santolina chamaecyparissus* and egg-yolk yellow. It has no unpleasant smell.

As with all Santolinas, the thread-like leaves do not last throughout the summer but hang on behind the younger leaves after they have wilted. Sometimes they hide themselves so tidily that they do not detract from the appearance of the shrub, but in certain years they make the foliage look dirty in late summer. When this happens, it is obviously better to shorten them back and force the plant to make a fresh start, but this does not necessarily have to be done at any special time for the young growth is particularly hardy and does not get damaged when caught by early frosts.

Spring pruning can be severe when necessary, for this is a variety which will break from hard wood, but plants that have been over-pruned always seem clumsy and out of character for this should be a light and feathery shrub.

It can be increased in just the same way as *Santolina neapolitana* and is just as easy. Young plants are completely hardy but only grow into good bushes if they are kept well stopped during their first summer.

SENECIO *cineraria*

Origin: Mediterranean.
Habit: Upright shrub. Ht. 2′, allow 8″ between seedlings.
Hardiness: 4–5.
Use: Summer bedding.
Planting time: May.
Main pruning: May.
Propagation: Seed.

For generations, large quantities of *Senecio cineraria* have been used as dot plants in bedding displays and it is still possible to buy seedlings by the tray-full. These seedlings are probably as attractive as any other subject used for the purpose but they certainly do not even hint at the beauty of mature plants.

Like all other seedlings they vary in form and in hardiness, above all there is a big difference in the amount of felt carried by the young growth. With some, both the stems and the leaves of new breaks are almost white, while with others, it may take two or three weeks and a lot of sun before the leaves start to develop a covering of white felt.

When a seedling stands out as being particularly white, it is always worth watching, but it should be made to prove itself before it is used as a parent for many of the most beautiful seedlings turn out to be tender.

These bedding plants seldom need any special grooming once they have been stopped but in a hot season it is just possible that the occasional shoot may have to be cut back because it has run to flower. Selected specimens, left to overwinter in the garden, must be firmly pruned in May. Thereafter they can be treated in the same way as named cultivars.

From the flower decorator's point of view, pieces cut off un-named specimens of *Senecio cineraria* must always be suspect for they seldom take kindly to water and have a nasty habit of wilting without warning.

Most seed firms offer seed taken from named cultivars, such as 'White Diamond', but it must be emphasised that plants grown on from this seed are unlikely to carry all the characteristics of their parent and that therefore they should not be labelled with the name

of this parent. The only way of raising a plant with all the virtues of *Senecio cineraria* 'White Diamond', for example, is to start with a plant of 'White Diamond' and take a cutting from it.

However if a good seedling does appear and does survive, there is no reason why this plant should not be given its own name and this name could then be applied to all the cuttings taken from it.

Seed germinates well and can be sown, either in September or in early February, under glass. The young plants do best when they are potted into 3" pots as soon as they show their first two leaves. If necessary they can be grown in boxes but these seedlings are inclined to show signs of distress when they are put out in May, for it is impossible to dig the roots out of a box without doing some damage.

SENECIO *cineraria*

Origin:	Garden.
Habit:	Upright shrub. Ht. 30", allow 18"–24" width.
Hardiness:	4.
Use:	Border.
Planting time:	May.
Main pruning:	May.
Propagation:	Cuttings.

This cultivar was originally selected because its shoots kept well in water. It has proved, however, to be an extremely decorative garden plant though it is not as white as *Senecio cineraria* 'White Diamond'.

The leaves of 'Ramparts' are oak-shaped and often measure as much as 5" in length. Even when quite young, these leaves look as if they had been cut out of pale grey felt and then powdered with a fine white dust. How sharply this Senecio should be pruned depends on the amount of space available. If the plant has already filled up the area on which it stands, then it can be pruned drastically, but when there is room for expansion, it is really better not to be too severe,

PLATE IV

but rather just to cut back the previous year's growth to within two, or even three nodes.

After pruning the stumps cover themselves with shoots and if some of these were not stopped straight away, the result would be terribly crowded. Stopping half the shoots not only relieves the pressure but also ensures a useful reserve of foliage. By June, the plants should look like snowmen. Unluckily it is at this time that the flowering stems start to grow from the base and if these are allowed to run to bud they can spoil the whole effect. Luckily the flowers are very ordinary and nothing is lost if the stems are cut away just as soon as they are spotted. *Senecio* 'Ramparts' does not produce many flowering stems and this is a small job.

Removing the first lot of foliage when it has lost its lustre takes a little longer, however. From the point of view of the health of a plant, it need not be done, but when the beauty of a shrub is dependent on its leaves, it seems worth the effort of clearing away the old so that the new can be seen. This is generally done in late July and leaves the plant with a cover of young foliage which will carry it right through the winter.

The leaves are beautifully shaped and can be used in all sorts of different ways in flower arrangements. For small work it is quite unnecessarily extravagant to cut away a whole shoot, for individual leaves harden perfectly and can often be found with 3″ stems. The drill for hardening is to singe the cuts, and here it should be said that to singe does not mean to burn, and that more harm than good is done when the stems are held so long in the flame that they lose their shape.

Cuttings will root whenever they are taken but for convenience it is usual to take 4″ side shoots in July, root them in a sandy mixture under a cloche or large glass jar. Once rooted they must be potted and kept in a frame for the winter, for young plants take a time to make sound wood.

To build a good specimen shrub it is essential to stop the main shoot as soon as it is possible to take off the tip and leave three pairs of leaves. Thereafter each shoot must be stopped back in turn so that, by the end of July, the plant is carrying at least eight breaks.

SENECIO *cineraria*

Origin: Garden.
Habit: Round bushy shrub. Ht. 18″, allow 16″ width.
Hardiness: 4.
Use: Border.
Planting time: May.
Main pruning: May.
Propagation: Cuttings.

It is sometimes difficult to realise that *Senecio cineraria* 'White Diamond' and *Senecio cineraria* 'Ramparts' are really two forms of the same species for they differ in so many ways. The leaf of 'White Diamond' for example, far from being oak-like, is pointed at the tip and very much smaller than that of Ramparts, and the shrub itself is so compact that, from a distance, it could well be mistaken for a snowball. The great distinguishing feature of this particular cultivar, however, is that each of its shoots is crowned with a flat diamond-shaped cluster of leaves. It is from this cluster that the flowering stems eventually emerge.

The young leaves of this cultivar are almost pure white but they turn to a soft grey with age. The effect, however, of the plant from a distance is white, for the young leaves show up extremely well.

In May, 'White Diamond' responds to the same kind of pruning and stopping as 'Ramparts' but needs slightly different treatment in July for 'White Diamond' has a great urge to flower and mere dead-heading does little to discourage this. Each rosette could, of course, be cut back as soon as it showed signs of producing a flowering stem, but this would mean that some very healthy foliage would have to be removed and that the plant would be left naked at the height of the season. If, however, the first few stems are just nipped out as they appear, leaving the rosettes intact, it takes a few more weeks before more appear and, by this time, the first crop of foliage is probably losing its brilliance and the second crop has advanced far enough to take over, so that pruning is not quite such a painful business.

Sprigs of 'White Diamond' will not keep in water until they are completely mature. As this occurs when the flowering stems start to show, prunings can sometimes be used in decorations.

The propagation of this cultivar is similar to that of 'Ramparts', but being a slower grower, it does not need so much stopping.

SENECIO *compactus*

Origin: New Zealand.
Habit: Small shrub. Ht. 30″, allow 16″ width.
Hardiness: 3.
Use: Border. Rockery.
Planting time: May.
Main pruning: May.
Propagation: Cuttings.

Senecio compactus might well be described as a very beautiful miniature *Senecio laxifolius*, though the white outline to its grey leaves is possibly even more sharply defined.

It is a graceful shrub, being slow growing and one that does not appreciate too much pruning. Its flowers are yellow and just as uninteresting as those of *Senecio laxifolius*, but luckily it does not try to flower very often.

It is an irritating plant to propagate. At times it is prepared to root magnificently but more often it fails dismally. The best results seem to stem from $1\frac{1}{2}$″ soft cuttings set on bottom heat in November. Though I have not tried myself, there seems to be no reason why it should not layer perfectly easily.

SENECIO *laxifolius*

Origin: New Zealand.
Habit: Shrub. Ht. 4′. Eventually spreads over a square yard.
Hardiness: 2–3.
Use: Border.
Planting time: April–May.
Main pruning: April.
Propagation: Layering. Cuttings in November.

If this shrub were either rare or difficult, its beauty would probably be better appreciated and it would receive the treatment it deserves. As it is, the majority of plants of *Senecio laxifolius* are lucky if they are pruned every third year and often have to carry a huge crop of unsightly seed heads.

This seems a waste of good material, for the foliage of this Senecio does not last for ever and becomes drab when old and sere. It is the contrast between the felty surface of the oval leaf and the white edge which is so attractive and this only really shows on young leaves.

In April it takes some courage to cut away the foliage which has been such a consolation throughout the winter, but spring pruning is essential for the health of a plant. How far to cut is a matter of choice. It is sufficient merely to shorten the current growth back to two nodes but does no harm to cut into the old wood, for this is a plant which breaks very freely.

There is, in fact, a danger that a particular plant may produce so many breaks that if some were not removed it would become a tight mass of leaves with neither shape nor form. By stopping some of the shoots when about 6″ long it is possible to avoid this kind of overcrowding and, at the same time, to ensure a reserve of young growth.

The flowering stems are whiter than the leaves and are remarkably attractive when in bud. The flowers themselves have little real beauty and go to seed almost as soon as they open. When this happens, every leaf loses its vigour immediately and the poor plant does not regain its pristine appearance until it has grown a completely new cover of young foliage.

Plants that have had their flowering stems removed before the flowers open are always effective from August onwards provided the whole of the stems were cut away and not merely the top clusters, for shrubs that have been prevented from flowering make Herculean efforts to make fresh buds and these always develop on the old stems.

Young plants, in their first summer, need training for they are inclined to straggle and become leggy. By stopping each shoot in turn back to two nodes it is usually possible to build up a sound little bush with plenty of breaks before the beginning of August when stopping, of course, has to cease.

The one way of killing *Senecio laxifolius* is to cut it about in winter, though just a few pieces can be taken if they are carefully chosen and their removal does not leave a nasty hole. Young breaks will result from any cut, but if they are well covered with shoots and foliage when they emerge they will not suffer. When too much foliage has been taken and the stump is left exposed, however, any break which does appear is bound to get frosted.

Sprigs taken from *Senecio laxifolius* will harden perfectly in hot water once they are mature, but it is always difficult to find any long stems on properly pruned plants and, for this reason only, it pays to grow a few unpruned specimens just for the sake of cutting.

The difference in appearance between *Senecio laxifolius* and *Senecio greyii* is too slight for the average gardener, as opposed to botanist, to appreciate, but it is always said that *Senecio laxifolius* is much hardier than *Senecio greyii*. Some years ago, however, some cuttings of *greyii* were sent to me from New Zealand and proved themselves hardier than *laxifolius*, so it would seem that there is very little difference between the two species.

Beautiful little plants can be produced by layering and this is certainly a very quick and easy way of producing a sizeable specimen. Cuttings root best on bottom heat in November.

SENECIO *leucostachys*

Origin:	Patagonia.
Habit:	Small shrub. Ht. 2′, allow 18″ width.
Hardiness:	4.
Use:	Border.
Planting time:	May.
Main pruning:	May.
Propagation:	Cuttings.

When seen at its best, *Senecio leucostachys* is probably the loveliest of all the small silver shrubs for its foliage is both white and delicately cut. Unfortunately it does not produce a lot of felt when growing freely and is inclined to become coarse. This is always liable to happen in a damp muggy summer.

Experience has shown that *Senecio leucostachys* needs to be slightly starved and that when its roots are confined within a 6″ pot, the foliage keeps white throughout summer and autumn and seldom becomes too lush.

Although not considered to be really hardy, it can withstand 25 degrees of frost when grown hard, but many winter casualties are caused by wind damage. Patagonia may be the windiest country in the world but this species must surely come from a nicely protected corner for it is incredibly brittle and will not survive a winter in the garden if it is not carefully tied. Some gardeners throw a single piece of string netting lightly over their plants and tie this in loosely. This trick works well provided the piece of net used is not too large and the job is done carefully so that there is no bunch of net at the base which might become sodden and damage the bark.

The loose flat clusters of creamy flowers are rather pleasant and, as the plant is always busy making fresh growth, there is no point in removing these until they start to set seed. It is essential, however, to cut away the entire flowering stem when dead-heading and at the same time to shorten back all lanky growth. If this is done before the beginning of August, the plant has time to fill itself out with new growth, and compact specimens always get through the winter much better than those which are loosely knit.

Whether established specimens of *Senecio leucostachys* should be heavily pruned in May is somewhat debatable but must, in the long run, depend on the plants themselves. When they have been carefully trained and stopped in their first year, the main branches should be standing reasonably upright, but if a branch has been damaged during the winter, it may well be found lying parallel to the ground. This sort of branch cannot carry a weight of foliage and is always liable to split, so it is better to saw it off at pruning time. On the other hand, one of the charms of this species is that it is graceful and once plants have been cut back too hard they can become very clumsy.

There is no grey foliage that will keep in water as long as a well chosen piece of *Senecio leucostachys*, but to do this it must have a hard stem and finely cut white leaves. Soft rank growth wilts as soon as it is cut. Stems must always be sealed with a flame.

Although cuttings of this variety will root in July in the garden, young plants are not hardy, so it is easier to take cuttings in early spring and root them on bottom heat. These grow very fast and March cuttings are always ready for their first stop before being put out in May.

STACHYS *lanata*

Origin: Caucasus to Persia.
Habit: Ground-covering perennial. Stem 12″, allow 8″ width.
Hardiness: 2.
Use: Front edge of border.
Planting time: March–April.
Propagation: By division.

Stachys lanata, Lamb's Lugs, must surely be one of the best loved of all English plants, if one is to judge by the number of names it has collected. There are far too many to be quoted and most compare the leaf to the ears, tail or tongue of some animal, but country folk in the North seem to me to have a better idea, for they know it as Baby's Flannel or Jesus' Flannel.

Stachys lanata is a thoroughly good tempered plant for the front edge of a border, but just because it is so good tempered is no reason why it should be neglected, for a little grooming is very well repaid. The best season for the long woolly leaves is in June, before the spikes have started to run. At this time they are completely covered with a thick woolly down but they do not seem to produce any more of this down as they lengthen so the cover gradually seems to get thinner. By the end of July the early leaves have lost their vigour, but if the spikes are cut down, there should be quantities of young leaves waiting in the wings. By pulling off the old foliage, the new growth is given a chance to expand and plants that have been properly stripped in July can be quite lovely by mid-August. The flower stems themselves are completely covered with wool and carry several pairs of woolly leaves. The little mauve flowers come in whorls round the stem but are almost hidden and certainly cannot be seen at a distance.

Gardeners often complain that *Stachys lanata* harbours slugs and this is very true if the old leaves are allowed to rot away into a slimy mess. Overcrowding also leads to an infestation of slugs and this is a subject which should really be re-planted every second year.

Many flower decorators like using a group of *Stachys lanata* flowers in large arrangements, but they have the maddening habit of chasing the sun, and I would think that the real value of this Stachys is as a source of good leaves to use inside small designs. These leaves cut perfectly and never go limp, whether they are cut singly or as rosettes.

Propagation is, of course, by division which can be done either in autumn or in spring. The best pieces to choose for re-planting are those which grow on the outside of the old plant and have three or four breaks. They should always be detached by hand.

STACHYS 'Silver Carpet'

Origin:	Garden.
Habit:	Ground-covering perennial. Allow 8″ width.
Hardiness:	2.
Use:	Front of border.
Planting time:	March–April.
Propagation:	Division.

Stachys 'Silver Carpet' came to light when a customer complained to a nurseryman that her plants of *Stachys lanata* never tried to flower. It was then discovered that her plants were something quite different, but nobody has yet been able to identify it as it has still not produced a flower.

However, it is a very useful plant for those who do not want to have the smooth edge of a border suddenly broken up with flowering spikes and though its leaves are not quite as woolly as those of *Stachys lanata* in early summer, they usually keep in condition for a longer period. As with *Stachys lanata*, so with 'Silver Carpet' the plants must be kept clean and all dirty foliage removed.

The one weakness shown by 'Silver Carpet' is that the leaves of established plants are inclined to become mottled by mildew in a dry season. This does not seem to happen to young plants, and I cannot help thinking that the disease is encouraged by overcrowding, for there is no question that this variety produces far more shoots and leaves than *S. lanata* and that it is obliged to pack them together into a very tight mass. So it would seem that the old plants should be dug up every autumn and divided.

For the flower decorator the advantage of 'Silver Carpet' is that it has longer leaves than *S. lanata* and that these all come on 4″ stems, but the disadvantage is that they do not mature till mid July, and that they will not take water when soft. Nevertheless it is worth having in the cutting border, for it does produce some very good leaves in August and September when other foliage is becoming difficult to find.

TANACETUM *densum amanum*

(*Chrysanthemum haradjanii, C. poterifolium*)

Origin: Turkey.
Habit: Mat-forming perennial. Ht. 6". Spreads over 9" in first year.
Hardiness: 3.
Use: Front of border. Rock garden.
Planting time: May.
Propagation: Cuttings. Rough layers.

There are several of these superb carpeting Tanacetums, this being the one most usually seen. It spreads out into a dense white mat of rosettes, made up of little white feathery leaves which look much like baby ostrich feathers. These begin to show on established plants in March and are nearly white from the start. The mats are at their best in June when they look just like woolly rugs. In late July the lower leaves begin to go yellow but these can be hidden if a new crop of shoots is encouraged by judicial cutting.

This Tanacetum is a very good example of a plant having outstanding foliage and wretched flowers, for the leaves are beautiful, whether seen under a microscope or from a distance, and yet the flowers are no better than those of the common groundsel. Luckily it does not flower every year.

Although individual specimens of this Tanacetum will survive for many years, it is better to re-plant every third year for the plants tend to leave the ground as they age and become very untidy. Many 'miniature' enthusiasts use the leaves and tiny rosettes in their work, which indicates that they will keep in water, but this is not really a plant for the cutting border for its value is limited.

Propagation can be by layers which are very easy in summer or by cuttings which strike without difficulty in summer if they are well dusted with Orthocide when they are inserted. Without this precaution there is always a danger of botrytis (grey mould) which attacks the leaf and works its way up into the stem.

The best cuttings are fairly young shoots which have developed sufficient leaves to form rosette-like tops. They can be taken with or without a heel but must be short-jointed and not more than $2\frac{1}{2}''$ in length. Lanky cuttings seldom make good plants.

As with *Artemisia lanata* there are several forms of *Tanacetum densum amanum*. Of these the most satisfactory seems to be the one previously known as *Chrysanthemum poterifolium*, which is extremely tough and remains tidy for years on end.

TEUCRIUM *fruticans*

Origin:	Southern Europe.
Habit:	Shrub. Ht. 5′, allow for $3\frac{1}{2}'$ width.
Hardiness:	4.
Use:	Against South-facing walls.
Planting time:	May.
Main pruning:	After flowering.
Propagation:	Cuttings.

This is a shrub which really does enjoy a thoroughly arid position and, though *Teucrium fruticans* can be grown on most South-facing walls, it thrives best when planted right under the over-hanging eaves of an Elizabethan house. When conditions are right, it is extremely vigorous and forces up a great number of thin stems. These are white and carry glistening silver leaves. The main crop of pale mauve flowers usually opens in May, but after a hot summer, there is sometimes a second flush in September.

Although established plants have to be controlled, *Teucrium fruticans* is not improved by severe pruning, and it is better not to touch it until after it has flowered in summer, when the flowering growth can be shortened back.

It is not a particularly useful plant to grow for flower decoration for when the stems are cut there is so much space between the leaves that they look bare. Moreover, these stems tend to wilt in water unless they are woody at the base. This unfortunately does not happen until autumn, when cutting would damage the plant in any case.

Teucrium fruticans is not easy to strike from soft wood, although semi-mature cuttings will root in late summer if taken with a heel and set in a sandy compost. Young plants raised in this way must be protected for their first winter. Another way of propagating is by layers, but this involves training a few shoots down towards the ground while they are pliable in spring. The shoots to choose are those that grow low down on the plant and show no signs of flowering. These are usually ready in June, and it probably pays to peg them down into 4½″ pots plunged into the ground so that they can be lifted in autumn, for newly rooted layers of *T. fruticans* are not very hardy and cannot be left in the open ground for the winter.

TEUCRIUM *pulverulentum*

Origin: —
Habit: Low spreading perennial. Ht. 8″, allow 8″ width.
Hardiness: 3.
Use: Front edge of border. Rockery.
Planting time: April. May.
Propagation: Layers. Cuttings.

This is one of the best grey plants for the front edge of the border for it stays remarkably silver throughout the summer and needs no special attention. The little leaves, about ¾″ in length, are so densely felted that it would be worthy of a prominent position in any garden, but its beauty is not entirely dependent on its leaves, for the little heads of rosy-mauve flowers have considerable charm and they appear throughout the season.

It needs very little pruning, and keeps perfectly tidy if the old growth is shortened back in May.

Teucrium pulverulentum can be layered very easily if a lead can be found which has not gone to bud. Cuttings root best on bottom heat in June and should not be more than 2″ in length.

VERBASCUM *bombicyferum* (Mullein)

(*Verbascum broussa*)

Origin: Asia Minor.
Habit: Biennial. Ht. 5', allow 14" width.
Hardiness: 2.
Use: Back of border.
Planting time: September–November.
Propagation: Seed.

Most of the grey-foliaged subjects suitable for the back of the border are either grey or glaucous rather than silver or white. This makes *Verbascum bombicyferum* particularly valuable, for though the florets which surround the tall spikes are pale yellow they only open spasmodically, and it is the stem, which might well have been made out of a roll of cotton wool, which shows up from a distance.

Many gardeners do not get the best out of this Verbascum because they forget that it is monocarpic and starts to die as soon as it has ripened a few pods, so they leave the main spike to grow up and up until they are left with 2' of seed heads and about half a dozen flowers on top. This is wrong, for the seed heads are very ugly and while they are left on the plant there is always a danger of sudden collapse. By cutting away the spike before too many pods have formed the vigour of the plant is conserved so that it is able to throw all its energy into making strong side shoots. These produce a superb display in August and September.

Flower decorators often find that, though there should be many uses for the flowering side shoots, these curl towards the light. To a certain extent the spikes can be kept straight if they are rolled in newspaper before being placed in a bucket to harden. When the whole of the main stem is cut it may be found to be hollow, and, if so, will need filling with water and plugging before hardening. It is the bottom leaves of young plants which are particularly useful, however, for they make excellent centres for designs of all sizes, and by sowing a few seeds whenever possible one can ensure a succession of good leaves in winter as well as in summer. These have very short stems, however, and it often pays not to cut off the leaves but to pull up the whole plant. This is not too painful when the seedlings have been grown for the purpose.

Verbascum bombicyferum is a very close cousin of the wild Mullein, and it is decidedly promiscuous. It is therefore extremely difficult to keep the seed 'clean' and there will always be a number of rogues in every batch of seed. These can be detected by their second pair of leaves which are always greener and slightly larger than they should be.

Seed will germinate if sown in the garden in summer, and when plants are needed for border display, this should be done in July. Under glass, seed sown in early February produces suitable seedlings for planting out in May.

VERBASCUM *olympicum*

Origin:	Western Anatolia.
Habit:	Monocarpic. Ht. 7'–8', allow 2' for flowering specimens, 14" for those grown as ground cover.
Hardiness:	2.
Use:	Flowering spikes for the back of the border. Immature plants in their second year as ground cover.
Planting time:	Autumn or early Spring.
Propagation:	By seed.

Although *Verbascum olympicum* has many features in common with *Verbascum bombicyferum*, it is a very different plant. To begin with it takes two full years instead of one to reach maturity. Then it is taller than *Verbascum bombicyferum*, much more floriferous and its flowers are golden rather than pale yellow. Even its leaves are longer and more pointed, and instead of coming into flower on a single spike, it always surrounds its main spike with a mass of side shoots which come into flower at the same time, so that the effect is that of a giant candelabra.

A well grown specimen of *Verbascum olympicum* is a magnificent sight when at its peak, and with discreet dead-heading it can be kept in flower from early June through to late August. The effect, however, of such a plant is essentially yellow rather than silver.

The great rosettes of grey leaves which it makes in its second year are quite different, however, for they are heavily felted and most

impressive when grouped together in the border. The only disadvantage of using the plants in this way is that if the rosettes are left
in situ for another year they will undoubtedly run up to flower and
would probably be horribly out of place. So the groups have to be
replaced each autumn.

However, *Verbascum olympicum* is as easy to raise from seed as
Verbascum bombicyferum and, in fact, there are gardeners who sow
seed every year in order to have a quantity of young plants to use as a
ground cover, for there is no weed capable of making a nuisance of
itself under such heavy leaves.

VERONICA *incana*

Origin:	Southern Europe.
Habit:	Mat-forming perennial. Allow 12″ width.
Hardiness:	3.
Use:	Edge of border.
Planting time:	April.
Propagation:	Division.

This Veronica is certainly a plant for the true connoisseur for, though
it never grows into a very big specimen, yet it forms a perfect
carpet-like mat of neatly packed leaves which keep surprisingly clean
throughout the summer. These mats make an excellent base for the
dark blue flower which comes in late July. The spikes are nearly 14″
in length, of which the top 6″ is always covered with dark blue
flowers.

Veronica incana, like so many other treasures, is not completely
reliable and has a nasty habit of disappearing during the winter. All
my experiences have suggested that it is hardy enough, but that slugs
find it delicious and gobble up the shoots as they emerge. Cuttings
do not strike easily but this Veronica can be increased by division in
March.